TABLE OF CONTENTS

CHAPTER 1

INTRODUCTION

> Secretary of Defense Donald Rumsfeld dismissed the citizen-soldiers of the pre-AVF era as "adding no value, no advantage, really, to the United States armed services.[1]
>
> Andrew J. Bacevich, *The New American Militarism*

The liberation of Iraq in 2003 and the occupation of Germany in 1945 are two of the major nation-building efforts undertaken by the United States in recent history. These nation-building efforts have occurred because of an extremely destructive war or due to mismanagement by the ruling regime that had adversely affected the safety and well being of the civilian populous. The topic of this thesis is to compare and analyze the successful occupation and rebuilding of Germany, as implemented in the Marshall Plan, from 1945 to1948 after the end of World War II and to contrast that to the occupation and rebuilding of Iraq, after Operation Iraqi Freedom, from 2003 to 2005.

This thesis is to determine if the United States and coalition forces are on the road to success for Iraq to modernize the society, culture, and economy, much as what the United States was able to accomplish for Germany. Reconstruction will eventually allow the nation to integrate as an equal partner with the nations of the world. What methods and plans were implemented that insured that the rebuilding of Germany was successful, and why have appropriately similar measures not been taken in Iraq?

There are many similarities between the rebuilding of Iraq and the rebuilding of Germany. Agreements, on how to proceed, between the military and the politicians are as crucial as the support of the people in both the occupied and occupying nations. The military is traditionally the best-equipped and prepared organization in the United States

1

to conduct reconstruction. In Germany, this was due to the large numbers of Soldiers that had been drafted and were available. In Iraq, the military is the only governmental organization that has the manpower and funds to conduct this type of mission.

This thesis will focus on the analysis utilizing a construct based upon the diplomatic, informational, military, and economic (DIME) aspects of the nations reviewed. This method will allow an analysis of the differing components and contrasts of the occupation of the two nations. Some of the questions that will be asked are described under the different headings of DIME below.

Diplomatic, Informational, Military, and Economic

Diplomatic Means

An analysis of the varying Diplomatic Means utilized in Germany and Iraq will determine if the decisions made and the policies enacted were correct. The basis for successful reconstruction is a strong and effective government. If fair and impartial laws, applying to all, do not exist then trust and belief in the government will not exist in the populous. Some of the questions that will be researched under the Diplomatic means are:

Was there a marked difference in governing styles between the two nations based on maintaining the Nazi infrastructure to continue running Germany to the removal of the Ba'athists from Iraq? The intent of looking at de-Nazification versus removal of the Ba'athists is to determine if the total removal of the Ba'athists, all at once, in the beginning of the liberation severely hampered the ability of the United States and the coalition to quickly put Iraq on the road for successful reconstruction. The alternate was to follow the policy utilized in post World War II Germany, which favored a gradual phasing out of the Nazi's in key governmental positions. This is a key issue as the

Ba'athists and the Nazis had permeated the entire society from the government, to education, to industry and the military.

What was the effect of the creation of the Iraq constitution to the effects generated by the German constitution? After the liberation of Iraq, self-rule was relatively quickly reestablished to a selected, and then elected, group of officials. Germany took much longer to gain autonomous power as the occupying powers phased in responsibilities on a much slower period. The two respective constitutions had very similar points that they addressed. The freedom to vote, for women to gain an education, and the establishment of a fair democratic system are just a few.

Was there a differing in the effects between the problems encountered through de-Ba'athification and de-Nazification? As mentioned above de-Ba'athification was accomplished with a rapidity that generated many problems that had not been initially expected. The slow phasing out of the Nazis seemed to cause less turmoil in the operation of the nation and with increased confidence in the population. This seems to have led to more stability in 1945 Germany than has been seen in 2005 Iraq.

Was there a marked difference, or similarity, in popularity among the peoples of America, Germany, Iraq, and among the international community for the Marshall Plan versus the implementation of the Iraq rebuilding plan? The support for or against the proposed projects in both countries played heavily on the support given to the rebuilding nations and the level of freedom with which they were allowed to rebuild. Research will determine how the level of popularity adversely affected the ability of the occupying and liberating forces in conducting their missions.

Did this popularity differ among the governments, population, and militaries of the involved nations? Determination of the popularity levels among the different governments, tribes, and religions can have a significant effect on the political, economic, and military support given to the rebuilding efforts. As the American military was the largest force provider involved in both nations rebuilding, the support of the people and the politicians directly affects the effectiveness of the programs. If one of the three types of support listed above, political, economic, and military, is not consistent with the others, this would hinder all of the support provided.

Informational Means

The successful use of Informational Means is a combat and policy multiplier. Effective utilization of press, media, Internet, and other means has the potential to sway the fence-line supporters to the occupiers cause and mitigate the influence of the enemy. Some of the questions that will be researched under the Informational means are:

Was there differing types and amounts of Civil Affairs and psychological operations utilized on the civilian populations such as the use of radio, newspapers, media, television, and various public forums? The effect that Civil Affairs units and psychological operations have on the populations of Iraq and Germany can help or hinder the amount of support and level of success achieved in the rebuilding efforts. The media's ability to influence the nations supporting the coalition or at the least dissuade those that may become involved on the side of the enemy becomes critical when attempting to pacify a nation.

How were the media resources of radio, newspaper, and television utilized to influence public opinion of the garrisoning and rebuilding efforts in both nations? The

4

use of media sources as a propaganda tool and an informational source in war and peacetime is common. The media's success or failure may have a large impact on the level of cooperation among the target population. The ability to rally the people to a particular topic or to highlight the success of a project many often times will win more converts than increased force of arms.

Was there a differing level of popularity among the American, German, Iraqi, and international community in their governments, populace, and militaries and what support existed for the installed local and national governments? Success of the media in supporting the aims and goals of the occupying nations to put their own message to the people often influences the amount of resistance experienced in the governing of the occupied nations. The perceived support of the interim governments of Iraq and Germany and the desire and ability of the people to participate in the government is a key policy issue that the United States has espoused and guided in both nations.

Military Means

During reconstruction efforts use of the military in its role as the warfighter should not be the primary focus. The use of those forces to conduct medical and engineer civilian action programs can often provide larger benefits than combat patrols. This requires senior military and civilian leaders to avoid using the combat forces as the hammer to fix all of the problems and to think of more effective uses for them. Some of the questions that will be researched under the Military means are:

Comparing the numbers of troops left as garrison forces, their structure, mission and strength? The number and type of military forces left as the occupying forces in Germany in 1945, may have affected the formation of an insurgent force. The difference in actions against the two nations, liberation of Iraq versus the occupation of Germany, may have caused a significant impact in the mission type of the American forces and how the mission was ultimately prosecuted. The state of the occupied nation may also have attributed to the level of resistance that was experienced.

Germany had been involved in World War II since 1939 and through the prosecution of that war had sustained significant amounts of damage to the national infrastructure and to the population. At the end of World War II, saw the German population severely depleted due to the use of allied airpower. Healthy war age males were few in number and greatly out numbered by similar aged females. Iraq on the other hand had only experienced short durations of combat operations but still experienced massive amounts of damage to the infrastructure through neglect. The Iraqi male population was almost completely intact and in good health.

How were police and National Guard forces created and when were they given freedom to conduct operations? The foundation of law and order in any nation is the creation and implementation of the police forces and legal processes. The ability and existence of the National Guard creates a peace of mind that is also important to the smooth operation of the nation. The creation, funding, and mission set of the police and National Guard forces will determine their ability to respond to threats within the society domestically and to create a credible deterrent to outside influences on the nation.

After the formal cessation of hostilities following World War II, what were the various terrorist acts committed and the number of Soldiers injured or killed by them? The occupation of Iraq has brought to the American military a style of conflict that has not been experienced in over forty years, since the Vietnam conflict. The use of improvised explosive devices (IEDs), vehicle borne improvised explosive devices (VBIEDs), and suicide bombers have become the mainstay of the enemy in the war of today. After the conclusion of a war, the remains of the conflict are very often readily available in the forms of ammunition caches and equipment stockpiles. These resources, unless quickly gathered or destroyed, come back to haunt the occupying power as they are later employed against them when an insurgency begins.

What methods were employed by the military to control or contain the nation such as the use of curfews, ration cards, restriction on travel, international banking and financing? Successful control of the populace can limit the number of incidents that occur after hostilities have ended. The increased freedoms for the Iraqi people and the speed in which they have been granted have led to the increased use of VBIEDs against the American forces. Restrictions on travel, freedom of movement, and access to international funds could stop an insurgency before it has even begun.

Economic Means

The focus of economic programs during the beginning of an occupation is on providing the necessities of life. The difficulty with providing these services lies with determining priority and supplying the funding to support the programs. In the later phases of the occupation, judicious use of these funds in conjunction with information operations can win over many allies to the occupier's side. Some of the questions that will be researched under the Economic means are:

What amount of funds were spent and on what types of projects were they spent on? The influx of funds can radically alter the perceptions of the people the occupying powers are trying to influence. Where the money goes can say much about the intentions of the occupying powers. The money can go to industry to create an economically viable nation or it can go into public programs such as sewer, water, and trash collection to better the life of the populace. The occupying powers have a significant impact on where and how much of these funds are spent.

Was there a plan to continue national industries to generate foreign trade dollars, such as the rebuilding of the oil industry in Iraq or the Ruhr industrial capacity in Germany? The need to generate foreign trade dollars can offset the costs of an occupying power to donate funds for the well being of the populace and to offset the cost of the occupation itself. The ability to generate a positive trade balance can speed the reintegration of an occupied nation into successful competition with the world trade markets.

Who was responsible for oversight of the policies and enforcement of them? The military is traditionally the first, largest, and most prepared force on the ground to see to the initial needs of the occupied nation. At some point, the governance of the nation and the management of their economic interests must shift to a civilian body. This shift can be to an appointed body from the occupying power or to the legitimate government of the nation when they are prepared to assume the responsibility. This shift can take time and resources that are not initially planned for at the beginning of the occupation.

Limitations and Delimitations

The analysis of the occupation of Germany from 1945 to 1948, under the Marshall Plan, and the occupation of Iraq from 2002 to 2005 will utilize the diplomatic, information, military and economic (DIME) means perspective. The use of these four categories will give a comprehensive look into the many facets of the two occupations.

By utilizing the DIME perspective, comparisons and contrasts will be researched and correlations made between the two differing occupation missions that are separated by approximately sixty years.

This thesis will not analyze the Ba'ath and Nazi parties during their times in power in Germany and Iraq. Even though the two parties share many similarities, the analysis will only deal with the result of the removal of the two parties from power, after 1945 for the Nazis and after 2002 for the Ba'athists. Addressed further in the analysis will be the difference in the immediate removal of all Ba'athists from positions of authority and power, from the government, education, and the military, to the phased removal of the Nazis over a number of years.

Analysis of the religions and belief structure of the two nations will not be analyzed as the conflicts between fascism, as a religion and as a political party, is too interwoven together. The myriad versions of Islam are also not easily grouped together and with the beliefs of the insurgents placing them in the smallest minority of the Islamic groups, due to their radical beliefs. Currently, the government of Iraq is composed of some religious leaders in key positions and has been able to include representatives of the many variations of Islam and ethnicities that exist in Iraq today, from Christians, to Muslims, to the Kurds. On the other hand, the difference in culture and perception of the male populations will be analyzed.

This thesis will not discuss or analyze the war crimes tribunals that occurred in Nuremburg, Germany or the trials of Saddam Hussein and his henchmen. The trials did, and have not, significantly affected the occupation and rebuilding of the two nations. In Germany, the majority of the trials were held and tried by the military courts while the

9

trial of Saddam Hussein was tried in the civilian courts. The dissimilarity of the two situations precludes this aspect of the occupations from being analyzed here.

The disparity of the sexes that exists in Iraq today has begun to be overturned. Women now participate in the government as elected officials and in the field of education as teachers, they have also achieved the right to vote. This treatment of women has no correlation to the treatment of women in Germany from 1945 to 1948. As the Iraqi women experienced this discrimination prior to 2002, the subject has no bearing on this thesis.

Significance of the Study

The significance of this thesis is based on the current belief in American society that the Iraq War and the rebuilding of Iraq was to be a short process and that troops and funds would not be required to accomplish the mission. The average person has little knowledge of our nations past involvement with a foreign nation's rebuilding effort after war. Few understand the reasoning behind and importance of the garrisoning of troops in Germany, and that it still occurs today, sixty years after the end of World War II.

The intention of this research is to compare the success of the Marshall Plan and other rebuilding programs to the current data collected on the initial years of the Iraq occupation and rebuilding. The belief is that this line of research will be important to determine the initial success of the implemented programs and to give an estimate of the final outcome of the occupation and rebuilding of Iraq.

This research may also determine if the current existing force structure of the military is capable of handling this type of mission. This includes the numbers of units and men made available, the types of units utilized, and the identification if a clear plan existed that would guarantee success. Of these three, having a clear plan is the most

crucial.

---

[1]Andrew J. Bacevich, *The New American Militarism: How Americans Are Seduced by War* (New York: Oxford University Press, 2005), 219.

CHAPTER 2

HISTORIOGRAPHY

After the occupation, American policy makers determined that the rebuilding of

Germany was critical to the rebuilding of the remainder of Europe. Not just industry and

agriculture needed rebuilding but the societal structure needed to be changed. The

German governmental structure was so completely tied to Nazism that it crumbled along

with the party and military machines at the end of the war. The conquering forces were

required to operate essential services, have public utilities functioning, furnish a police

force, and establish fair and impartial courts.[1]

In a press statement released on 28 February 1947, former President Herbert

Hoover, as presidential envoy to Germany and Austria, states the governmental policy

towards rebuilding, "It may come as a great shock to American taxpayers that, having

won the war over Germany, we are now faced for some years with large expenditures for

relief for these people. Indeed it is something new in human history for the conqueror to

undertake."[2] This policy would cause the American Government to station millions of

troops and spend billions of dollars over the next sixty years to ensure its completion.

In April 1945, a Gallup Public Opinion Poll conducted dealt with this subject.

From Gallup Poll surveys taken, the majority of American citizens agreed with the policy

and the continued shortfalls that it would mean. The question dealt with providing aid to

Germany after the completion of the war: "For a year after the war in Europe is over

should people in the United States continue to put up with shortages of butter, sugar,

meat, and other rationed food products in order to give food to people who need it in

Europe?" 65 percent of respondents agreed, 8 percent were undecided, with only 27 percent in disagreement. The same question asked a month later had an agreement percentage of 85 percent, the no opinion percentage at 3 percent, and 12 percent for those who disagreed.[3]

This same level of support continued through the creation and implementation of the Marshall Plan, also known as the Economic Recovery Plan (ERP). Approval of the Marshall Plan occurred at the end of 1947, initiated in 1948, and dealt with the allocation of assistance to Europe to aid in rebuilding. Five Gallup Polls, consisting of two questions per poll, were conducted between July 1947 and November 1948. The first question asked if the person had heard of the Marshall Plan. The percentage stating yes rose from 49 percent in July 1947 to 82 percent in November 1948. The second question dealt with the approval level of the Marshall Plan. The results showed that fifty-seven percent of those polled approved of the plan.[4]

An alternate view of the support given to the Marshall Plan and rebuilding of Europe, was a Gallup Poll taken between 4 December 1945 and 9 December 1945. The purpose of this poll was to identify the way American citizens felt about the final disposition of Germany. The question asked, what do you think we should do with Germany as a country? The majority, 46 percent, wanted to supervise and control the nation, disarm the military, eliminate the Nazi's, and control the industries. President Truman initiated this program. What is surprising is that 34 percent of those surveyed wished to treat Germany very severely by destroying them as a political entity and economically cripple the country. This is a smaller difference between the two views than expected based on the previous Gallup Poll surveys on the acceptance of the plan. The additional 20 percent were either undecided or wished for the occupation to be more lenient.[5]

These results show that even though the Marshall Plan was popular, the outlook for a healthy German nation was anything but certain. This lack of support, demonstrated in the previous Gallup Poll question, shows that President Truman's policy was not whole-heartedly accepted by the American people. This led to harsh criticism in the press, as many wished to see the rebuilding of the American economy as the priority. It was not until the threat of Soviet expansion became real that the majority of Americans accepted the policies of the Marshall Plan.

One dominant feature of the American policy toward Europe was the principle that American and worldwide economic recovery depended upon the revival of the peacetime business, industry, and standards of living in Europe.[6] This philosophy fit in well with in the economic role Germany filled prior to World War II. Before 1939, Germany was an industrial powerhouse exporting manufactured items throughout Europe, Africa, and America. The loss of Germany's industrial capability severely hampered the reconstruction efforts in Europe. Repatriations in the form of factory equipment and resources to Britain, France, and Russia also complicated matters.

The need to maintain a garrison in Europe and to guarantee American interest in the future affairs of Europe was initially addressed by Secretary of State James F. Byrnes at Stuttgart on 6 September 1946. He stated that security forces would probably have to remain in Germany for a long time and that America would provide those forces for as long as needed.[7] Even then, the administration was addressing the future threat the Soviet Union represented.

The emplacement of military forces in Germany was to control a conquered civil population and to enforce the terms of surrender. The rising belligerence of the Soviet Union began to change this belief as the American Army moved more and more into the mold of an outpost in Europe for the enforcement of national policy.[8] Therefore, the American military, in cooperation with the British and French, were going to need to turn Germany into a buffer zone to hold back Soviet expansion further into Western Europe.

On 17 March 1948, in a speech to Congress, President Harry S. Truman proclaimed, "It is of vital importance, for example, that we keep our occupation forces in Germany until the peace is secure in Europe."[9] This speech set the stage for the continuation of American presence in Europe continuing into the twenty-first century. This speech occurred almost three years after the conclusion of World War II and was required due to the war of nerves over Berlin, which was growing tenser daily. Swiftly, it became apparent that the Soviet Union had selected the German capital as the scene for a test of power in their conflict with the West.[10] The Western nations would prove, with the Berlin Airlift that they would not back down or be cowed by threats. This conflict would be the first of many in the struggle between communism and democracy that would arise over the next fifty years.

In the intervening years between World War II and Operation Iraqi Freedom numerous policy changes occurred. In Korea, the United States participated as a part of the United Nations effort to repel the North Korean and communist Chinese forces. Even though, much like Germany, forces remain garrisoned there through the twentieth and into the twenty-first century, an actual occupation did not occur. Funding and aid had been provided over the years but no part had been forcibly occupied by the United States military at anytime.

Those that fought during the Korean Conflict either had served during World War II or had been teenagers. The average American viewed the evil of communism as spreading across the world and believed it needed to stopping. This was the first open conflict involving clashing armies of the Cold War, but it was relatively small scale and did not involve the number of draftees utilized previously or in Vietnam. In addition, this conflict did not last as long as the Vietnam War so the social weariness that is seen with longer conflicts did not come into play.

Much like the Korean Conflict, the Vietnam War was not an occupation by American forces. The Vietnamese government, like the Korean government, requested the aid of America to defeat the communist insurrection and external aggression. Vietnam, on the other hand, was a war fought by the children of World War II and Korean Conflict veterans. The key reason that America withdrew from Vietnam was the loss of the will of the American people, lack of observable strategic military success, and daily portrayal of the war in the living room. The war had stretched on for too long and the use of free media to bring the horrors of the war home was more than the American people could tolerate.

Vietnam was a continuation of the style of fighting that had started in the Korean Conflict. Communist forces saw that American firepower could very often defeat the human wave style attacks they espoused. In order to overcome this advantage, and due to the large amount of assistance being provided by the communist Chinese advisors, many of the tactics utilized were similar to those used by the Maoist forces in their war with the

Chinese Nationalist military. Tactics included utilizing hit and run attacks, terror attacks to turn the will of the populous, and the exploitation of the Vietnamese governments' lack of equal representation for all of the people.

The philosophy behind the invasion and occupation of Iraq is much different than was seen during World War II, the Korean Conflict, or the Vietnam War. Ambassador L. Paul Bremer stated in a meeting towards the end of his tenure as head of the Coalition Provisional Authority (CPA), "Mr. President we have to deal more effectively with the security situation. The intelligence is just not good. And I'm personally persuaded that the military has a strategy to win."[11] This is in direct opposition to World War II where the Allied forces had begun planning in 1943 for the occupation of Germany to commence at the conclusion of the war.

Anthony Cordesman, national security analyst for ABC, lists some of the mistakes made by the administration in the occupation and garrisoning of Iraq. First, was the military's plan for a premature withdrawal of troops instead of the anticipation of conducting stability operations. This goes back to ease and speed in which the first Gulf War and Operation Enduring Freedom (OEF) took place. Since the fall of the Soviet government, America had become complacent as the unchallengeable super power. Lulling the United States into a sense of complacency in its own superiority that has been shaken by events experienced during OIF.

The second point was the expediting of Iraq sovereignty before they were prepared. Iraq had suffered under one of the longest running dictatorships in modern history. Few of the citizens in Iraq could remember a time before Saddam Hussein's rule. This would complicate the transfer of authority to the Iraqi people. As Ambassador

17

Bremer pointed out, "Democracies don't work unless the political structure rests on a solid civil society . . . political parties, a free press, an independent judiciary, open accountability for public funds."[12]

The other difference that exists between World War II and Operation Iraqi Freedom (OIF) was that in World War II the whole nation of Germany was held responsible for the war and was occupied as such. In Iraq, President Bush declared that a liberation was taking place; this implies that a different set of rules would apply, with the holding of only one man responsible.

Declaring an occupation in Iraq would also alienate a number of Middle Eastern allies who were already marginally agreeing to the ousting of Saddam, as an occupation was not in their interests. Causing them to view the occupation as a repeat of the Christian Crusades and leading to an uproar among even liberal Muslims around the world. Fortunately, this did not occur as a coalition formed to prosecute the war and the United States did not act unilaterally.

The differentiation between liberation and occupation goes beyond a political reason. World War II cost the American people far more casualties than had been experienced in Iraq. The American family had had some one either wounded or killed in World War II or knew a family who had. In Iraq, this reminder of the cost paid is not as prevalent in American society.

American society is also much different. Prosecuting World War II required a large number of men to take the fight to Europe and Asia. This resulted in women being required to step out of traditional home making and assume what was then male roles within society, the factories, and even the military. This full commitment caused a tremendous shakeup in American society. Families planted victory gardens, women donated their pots and pans for the war effort, and the society under went hardship through rationing. The American society during OIF did not undergo any of these privations. Americans continued to shop and had not been required to go short on any of their comforts.

The advent of technology since World War II has also affected the belief that "boots on the ground" is secondary to what the latest machine can perform. Prior to OIF, the American military belief was that technology would compensate for shortfalls in personnel. The reliance on high technology satellites and unmanned aerial vehicles (UAV) tend to lead to a belief that a less technologically advanced force is an inferior one. This proved false. Another belief was that technology would offset numerical superiority and allow a unit to control, manage, and influence more territory with fewer personnel: also not necessarily true.

At the end of World War II, the four Allied powers split Germany into separate zones; America was responsible for a zone of 47,000 square miles with a population of 19,000,000. This breaks down to approximately 400 people per square mile.[13] In Iraq, United States forces controlled the majority of territory totaling 437,072 square kilometers (271,584 square miles) with a population of 27,499,638 (July 2007 estimate). This breaks down to approximately 101 people per square mile.[14]

The population of Germany had been severely depleted by the war. Women, children, and the elderly, outnumbered healthy uninjured men significantly. The area of Germany in the American zone that was not urban was viable farmland, which just needed to be farmed. In Iraq, the male population had not been depleted due to the war.

The relative number of civilian casualties had been light due to the use of technology (precision guided munitions as an example).

Religion also plays a role in the differences between the two situations. In Germany, the outlawing of religion and acceptance of fascism as the political philosophy of the state occurred. Fascism is a governmental system led by a dictator who has complete power. Germany saw few problems between religions at the end of World War II. Most of those who were not of the Nazi party had been sent out of the country or had been confined in the internment camps during the war. Incidents between the German populous and those who had been released from the camps were kept to a minimum by the American military.

In Iraq, the religious situation was much more difficult. The three major groups that exist, the Shia, Sunni, and Kurds, have been in conflict for a number of centuries. Not only is there religious conflict between the Sunni and Shia over the interpretation of the Koran, but there is cultural conflict against the Kurds. The schism between the Shia and Sunni has been occurring for so long that any chance at reconciliation seems improbable.

Cultural perspective is also an issue. In Germany, people identify themselves first as their family or surname, and then as Germans. Their national identity came second but they understand a strong cultural distinctiveness as German. Iraqi's do not have this perspective. Many view themselves as their family, then their clan, and then only as Iraqi's. Iraq, the nation, has only existed since the end of World War I when European colonialism began to recede. The nation was formed from a number of providences from the Ottoman Empire. The Iraqis never had a cultural identity or an experience to cause them to merge into one people.

Not only will the Iraqi people need to overcome the political barriers, which stand in their way, but also they will need to find a resolution for their religious differences. Neither problem will be easy to fix. As no separation of church and state exists as it does in the United States or other free nations, a compromise will need to be found that does not marginalize one people or group and allows fair representation for all. The influence of Iraq's neighbors also has an effect as each of those nations has its own interests for how Iraq turns out.

Due to the conflicts in Europe over the years, preceding World War II, Germany did not have the problem of dealing with contrary cultural and religious issues to as severe degree. The support of the United States for an independent Jewish homeland in the Middle East and its establishment, at the conclusion of World War II, averted many of the problems that face Iraq. As this action removed what could have been a disruptive influence on the reconstruction of Germany.

The occupation of Germany led to false expectations as to what America could accomplish. An article in the *New York Times* from June 1987 on the Marshall Plan illustrates this well. "But aid experts say the plan also raised unrealistic expectations. The plan created a false impression that we could solve any problem by throwing money at it.," said former Senate Foreign Relations Committee Chairman J. William Fulbright.[15] This belief has colored America's dealing with every situation since.

[1]"Occupation Forces in Europe, The First Year, 1945-1946, Volume 1," Office of the Chief Historian, European Command, August 1947: 106, Combined Arms Research Library, Ft. Leavenworth, KS.

[2]"Herbert Hoovers press release of The President's Economic Mission to Germany and Austria, Report #1, German Agriculture and Food Requirements," 28 February 1947.

[3]"The Gallup Poll Public Opinion 1935-1971" (Random House, New York, 1972), Survey # 344-K:500, 510.

[4]Ibid., Survey # 400-K:661, Survey # 406-K:683, Survey # 407-K:691, Survey # 412-T:715, Survey # 432-K:770.

[5]Ibid., Survey # 344-K:506

[6]"Occupation Forces in Europe Series, 1947-48, The Third Year of the Occupation Fourth Quarter, 1 April – 30 June 1948, Volume 1," Office of the Chief Historian, European Command, 1948:7, Combined Arms Research Library, Ft. Leavenworth, KS.

[7]"Occupation Forces in Europe, The Second Year, 1946-1947, Volume 1," Office of the Chief Historian, European Command, August 1947:21, Combined Arms Research Library, Ft. Leavenworth, KS.

[8]"Occupation Forces in Europe Series, 1947-48, The Third Year of the Occupation, Third Quarter, 1 January – 31 March 1948, Volume 1.," Office of the Chief Historian, European Command, 1948:1-2, Combined Arms Research Library, Ft. Leavenworth, KS.

[9]"Occupation Forces in Europe Series, 1947-48, The Third Year of the Occupation Fourth Quarter, 1 April – 30 June 1948, Volume 1," Office of the Chief Historian, European Command, 1948:106, Combined Arms Research Library, Ft. Leavenworth, KS.

[10]"Occupation Forces in Europe Series, 1947-48, The Third Year of the Occupation, Second Quarter, 1 October – 31 December 1947, Volume 1," Office of the Chief Historian, European Command, 1948:67, Combined Arms Research Library, Ft. Leavenworth, KS.

[11]L. Paul Bremer and Malcolm McConnell, *My Year in Iraq: The Struggle to Build a Future of Hope* (New York: Simon and Schuester, 2006), 228

[12]Ibid., 19.

[13]"Occupation Forces in Europe Series, 1947-48, The Third Year of the Occupation, First Quarter, 1 July – 30 September 1947, Volume 1," Office of the Chief Historian, European Command, 1948:2, Combined Arms Research Library, Ft. Leavenworth, KS.

[14]"Iraq," CIA World Factbook, https://www.cia.gov/cia/publications/factbook/geos/iz.html, 20 May 2007

[15]Ann Hughey, "The Lessons of the Marshall Plan," *New York Times,* 7 June 1987, 4.

CHAPTER 3

DIPLOMATIC MEANS

Government in Germany

Further research into *Occupation Forces in Europe, the First Year*, written by the

historians at the European Command Headquarters shortly after the events occurred.

They provided information on the initial interim governments established as the United

States was consolidating its hold on the German territories. Prior to the official surrender

of Germany on 9 May 1945, the Donitz government had taken hold of a large part of the

remaining German forces and territory.[1] Admiral Kurt Donitz was the ranking German

military officer remaining at the time of the surrender. He was allowed to be the

spokesman and primary representative for the German peoples, until the European

Command took him into custody on 24 May 1945 and initiated Plan Goldcup.

Plan Goldcup was to establish ministerial parties and control group to oversee the

occupation of Germany.[2] This allowed the United States military to have total control of

their territories. It is very similar to what occurred in Iraq in the beginning phases of the

operation, with the military taking control of the government and administering the

occupied territories.

Originally, the transfer from military to civilian command and control in Germany

was phased in over four months. The decision made was to speed this up to one month as

the German civilian government had completely broken down. The German people were

in shock and too stunned to offer much resistance to the occupying forces. The

government put in place was a civilian government headed by the theater commander

who also directed the occupation and employment of military forces in Austria. The decision as to who would administer the control of occupied Germany, the theater staff or the U.S. Group Control Council, was decided, by the allied nations in England, before the invasion of Europe took place.[3]

After the surrender of Germany, the occupation of the country did not occur all at once. As a tactical unit took command of a town or area, they were only required to do the bare minimum to establish law and order and relief for the inhabitants. Long-term occupation of these areas required specially trained personnel. These specialists had been recruited and trained for military governmental duties as part of the advanced planning for the occupation. The training focused on the administration of the conquered territories and on how to deal with the civilian populous. These personnel assumed responsibilities on the G5 staff and military government detachments.[4]

On 5 June 1945, a declaration by the allied forces stated that the central government of Germany was to disband. The allied powers were to provide for the administration of the nation.[5] Germany and Berlin were to be split among the allies into four zones. The western portions of Germany and Berlin were to divide into the United States, British, and French zones, while the east was to be the Russian zone. The civilian government in the United States zone of responsibility was the Office of Military Government United States (OMGUS).

The allied leaders once again met on 17 July 1945 at the Potsdam Conference. The key players of the allied forces attended, such as President Truman, Prime Minister Churchill, and Premier Stalin. The agreements reached during the conference covered some crucial political principles, such as the removal from political office of all Nazi's and punishment of all war criminals. The decision made was that no central German government was to be formed at this time. Decentralization of the political structure occurred through restoration of local self-governments based on democratic principles with encouragement of the participation of all political parties except the Nazi's. In addition, the commanders in the zones had absolute authority in their zone and all of the zonal representatives would act jointly in decisions affecting Germany as a whole.[6]

This structure remained in place for three years until 8 April 1948 when another conference took place to discuss a Federal Constitution for Germany. A report on a draft constitution was prepared and sent to the military governors of the four zones for their review.[7] Based on the results from the draft report a conference occurred in London in June 1948, attendees included the United States, Britain, France, Belgium, Netherlands, and Luxembourg. A general shape for the German government was agreed upon and an occupation statute was determined to be needed which would define the rights of the people.[8]

Because of the meeting in June 1948, three documents were presented to the elected German leaders on 2 July. The three documents were a proposed constitution, the occupation statute, and the proposition of the creation of a new German state. The German people were to have their own government but the Western powers reserved the right to interfere if the situation required. There were to be three functions of the government: the executive, legislative, and judicial. However, the allies would not cede power or responsibility for the control of foreign trade, foreign relations, level of industry, disarmament, and scientific research.[9]

On 8 July, the popularly elected German leaders returned with a counter proposal: instead of a constitution, they requested a statute. This was far less responsibility than the occupying powers were offering Germany. When it was explained to the German leaders that they were being offered more responsibility they rescinded their offer and accepted the option of the constitution.[10]

The political ideals agreed to during the Potsdam Agreement took shape very fast. Unlike Iraq, the Germans already had a tradition of elections and were able to conduct local elections relatively quickly after the end of hostilities. The first local free election occurred in Grosshessen on 20 January 1946, a little over eight months after the end of World War II.[11] Berlin was able to host municipal elections on 20 October 1946 and West German Constitutional Assembly elections occurred on 30 June 1946.[12]

The original plan for the governing of the American sector of Germany had OMGUS transfer from the military to civilian responsibility headed by the State Department, by 1 July 1948. The military had always recommended that it should relinquish the governing of Germany to a civilian organization. On 22 October 1947, the State Department said that temporarily they could not assume the responsibility. Thus on 23 March 1948, the State Department ceded the responsibility for the mission back to the military governor, General Lucius Clay.[13]

As the British and American zones began to merge through economics, other functions were identified that could be merged. On 9 February 1948 a German high court for the two economic areas was formed.[14] The merging of the judicial and economic fronts was in the initial scope of the Potsdam Agreement that all of the allied powers agreed to.

De-Nazification

One of the key decisions that came out of the Potsdam agreement was the removal of all Nazi's from power. Under the process of de-Nazification, in the American sector, all Nazi party funds and property was confiscated, it's records and headquarters were seized, and the parties leaders were arrested an interned. All Nazi schools were closed and newspapers and propaganda were prohibited. The youth groups, which still existed, also disbanded. Any Nazi laws that still existed were suspended; these laws primary dealt with discrimination. Due to this policy, by the end of 1945, 110,000 Germans were arrested and 80,000 civilians were in U.S. Army custody. [15]

De-Nazification began at the lowest levels of the government and included industry, non-governmental institutions, and the police. The initial declaration on the removal of all Nazi's from the government, prevented almost all incumbents from holding office. Few judges remained that had not been tainted, which affected the maintenance of law and order. If identification of an individual as a hard-core Nazi party member occurred, they were relegated to lowest clerical jobs and common labor as their only options for governmental work. The definition of hard-core members was those who profited from Nazi policies or participated in War Crimes. The OMGUS required that all Germans register as to their membership in the Nazi party. This allowed the government to identify and track past party members.[16]

De-Nazification of the German government and civil administration was complete in the American sector by June 1946. The basis of completion was on the removal of the hard-core Nazi members, identified by OMGUS, and replacement with competent individuals. The process of de-Nazification was so successful that by November 1945 the police, after having won the confidence of the military government, were to be issued

arms and ammunition. The police were officially de-Nazified by December 1945.[17]

OMGUS decided to turn the responsibility for de-Nazification over to the German

government on 5 November 1946. The concession to this expansion of their power was

that if satisfactory progress did not occur with in sixty days then OMGUS would

reassume responsibility for de-Nazification. After some delays, the German government

proved to OMGUS that they could deal with the responsibility and they remained in

charge of the program until its completion.[18]

Government in Iraq

Many of the problems that exist in Iraq today go back to the end of World War I.

At the conclusion of the war, Iraq was cobbled together from three provinces of the

former Ottoman Empire. This ad hoc nation came about from the results of a League of

Nations mandate under United Kingdom administration and the decline of European

imperialism.[19] In the south was the Shiite community, in the center the Sunnis, and in the

north the Kurds.[20] The fact that a European decree created the nation did not lend itself to

the stability of the nation through common desire or history, as is the case in Germany.

Ambassador Bremer's book, *My Year in Iraq: The Struggle to Build a Future of*

Hope, gives a very interesting insight into the diplomatic issues that faced the Americans

in 2003 and 2004 during his tenure as the administrator of the Coalition Provisional

Authority (CPA).[21] His work with the Governing Council and the Provisionary

Government is directly opposite of the occupation of Germany. In Germany, the military

government for a far longer period tightly maintained control.

The difference in the policies of the two occupations, Germany and Iraq, is related to the differing situations that led to the occupations. For one, in 1945 the United States and the allied powers had just completed a war that had counted millions as dead worldwide. In Iraq, President Bush declared that the coalition was a liberation force not a conquering army. Taking that view, the operational parameters for who was involved, civilian versus military, and what the level of their involvement is, was very different. Ambassador Bremer highlights this problem, "At the end of WWII, the United States and the other allies had clearly defeated the countries we had occupied. But here, I said, we've defeated a hated regime, not a country."[22]

Secondly, during the occupation of Germany, severe curtailment of the average person's liberties and freedoms occurred. In the case of Iraq, talks begin in June 2003 on elections and the formation of the governing council.[23] By the end of his book, Ambassador Bremer was already discussing the transfer of authority from the Governing Council to the interim elected government. This was less than two years after the official cessation of hostilities; in Germany, it took much longer until control transferred from the allied powers to the German officials.

At the beginning of 2004, a large amount of political pressure was applied by Congress, on the president and Ambassador Bremer, for Iraq to achieve self-governance by the end of 2004. The Department of Defense had also generated an interest in pulling troops out of Iraq before the spring rotation. This is a marked difference to the attitude and plans for the occupation of Germany. Due to the political pressure generated the CPA transferred sovereignty to the Iraqi's on 28 June 2004.[24]

30

From the review of the occupation reports, the military was the primary driving force in the governing of the American-controlled German zone. There are few references of the influence or interference by the State Department or other civilian organizations. The primary decision maker was the military.

This seems to be at direct odds with the military situation in Iraq. Most Commanders seem to operate within their areas generally following the theater commanders overall guidance. Nevertheless, these commanders have considerable freedom to operate or establish policies as they see fit. Many enact their own curfews and conduct their own operations with little coordination with other sectors. If one commander has a successful plan or policy it is only by chance that, commanders may hear of it and adopt it themselves.

Ambassador Bremer states that he was having many difficulties in working with other civilian agencies, "It was a sad reality that, while the president had ordered me to act with decisive speed, I was often hamstrung by organizations like the OMB and the State Department's Agency for International Development (USAID)."[25] During the tenure of the CPA, these difficulties were never rectified. This interference and work at cross-purposes did not occur in the recovery of Germany while it was under military control.

Where similarities exist between Germany and Iraq is the establishment of order and law in the nations. In Germany, one of the first steps taken was the United States disbandment of the Nazi special courts, traditional courts, and the suspension of particular Nazi laws.[26] Ambassador Bremer mentions that one of the first problems was to reestablish order with the use of law and the police.[27] Without local authority, a census to begin the democratic process was impossible.

Another similarity between Germany and Iraq was the amount of authority granted to the leadership on the ground to develop the strategic objectives for the rebuilding. Ambassador Bremer had his staff generate a plan for Iraq that consisted of five key objectives. The first was security as the priority with a strong and loyal police and army. The second was improvements in the lives of the average Iraqi. This included refurbishment of schools, establishment of electrical power to pre-war levels, and reopening of the hospitals. The completion of these accomplishments was set for 1 October 2003, within 90 days of the approval of the plan. The third was to get the oil production of the nation back to prewar levels, also to be finished within 90 days. The fourth objective was the establishment of a central bank to restart the economy. The fifth and final point was to prepare the groundwork for a representative government.[28]

The briefing of the plan to President Bush occurred on 4 August 2003 and approved, by him, for implementation that same day. Once the plan was approved, copies were made and sent to every representative and senator on Capitol Hill. The plan generated strong support from the Republicans but the Democrats say little. Later, when Ambassador Bremer returns to brief congressional leaders, influential members of the Democratic Party say they never saw the strategic plan sent to them on 23 July 2003.[29] This appears to be political wrangling by the Democrats to garner support from the American public.

Anthony Cordesman identified some strategic mistakes made by the United States during the occupation of Iraq. His most important point was that the United States failed to assess the lack of national identity, level of cultural differences, and scale of problems that would be encountered. The level of cultural differences was not just between the United States and Iraq but also between the varied cultures, tribes, and families in Iraq itself. The United States was also fundamentally wrong about how the Iraqi people would view the United States invasion.[30]

Cordesman also addresses the fact that the United States failed to create effective civilian elements to deal with nation building as it was never the intention to do so. The civilian force was ineffective due to the lack of personnel and that the majority stayed only for a short duration, typically three-month tours. The personnel assigned to the CPA typically had been vetted not on competence but on political and ideological leanings. These personnel were also unprepared to maintain governance of any sort due to not anticipating the possibility of the collapse of the Iraqi government.[31]

Cordesman identifies five elements of victory. These five elements are very similar to the strategic objectives listed by Ambassador Bremer, but look farther out on the time line of the rebuilding of Iraq. First, was the establishment of a pluralistic Iraqi government with a balance of power and security. The second was, to create an effective military, security, and police forces. The third element was, to provide aid, debt and reparations relief, and economic reforms. The fourth was, to develop a national consensus that legitimizes the new Iraqi government. The last element was to find a new balance with Iraq's neighbors.[32] These critiques ignore many of the basic problems that existed in Iraq during the first years of the invasion. He also did not list recommendations for solutions to these problems.

<u>De-Ba'athification</u>

On 16 April 2003, General Tommy Franks officially outlawed the Ba'ath party in Iraq. At the time, there were over two million members and the only way to become a teacher or a civil servant was to join the party.[33] This led to the removal a large number of Ba'athist who were not hard-core members but joined to make a living. The separation of the fanatic members from the others was to become a major problem much as de-Nazification had been. This highlights the problem of making sweeping policies without careful analysis of the consequences.

De-Ba'athification was to take many of the same steps that had occurred in Germany sixty years before. The scope and intent was to be the same with the banning of propaganda and portraits of Saddam Hussein, seizure of the party's headquarters and assets and the internment of their personnel. However, this process was to go much quicker and not be a phased process like that in Germany. The removal of all teachers, civil servant, and military members severely hampered the rebuilding efforts soon to be undertaken.

Before the incoming Iraqi government took power, supporters of the new leadership called for new and greater purges of the government and the Iraqi security forces in order to eliminate all Ba'athists. These plans would have affected all members' hard core and those who just went along to survive. This would also have caused tensions and driven a dividing line between the Sunnis and the Shiites as violence between the two groups continued to grow.[34]

Different from what occurred during de-Nazification, Cordesman states in his book, *Iraq Security Forces: A Strategy for Success*, "The Ba'ath party did not dissolve

34

when the CPA formally abolished it in May 2003. It reorganized with a new structure, established a new Politburo in 2004, and at least some elements operated from a de facto sanctuary in Syria."[35] In 1945, the Germans did not have a sanctuary to go to, reorganize, and recover from the war. Hitler was dead and the party died with him. In Iraq, Saddam Hussein was imprisoned and tried in an Iraqi court by Iraqi judges, but a number of his senior leaders escaped and have avoided capture.

Another issue with eliminating the Ba'ath party was that many full and part time members of groups and cells are linked by tribe, family, and locality. These ties may provide money, aid, and leadership to those who remain. Former members may also have access to funds from the former regime.[36] These deep running ties with family will be difficult to root out in the tribal system that exists in Iraq.

---

[1]"Occupation Forces in Europe, The First Year, 1945-1946, Volume 1," Office of the Chief Historian, European Command, August 1947: 2, 19, 20, Combined Arms Research Library, Ft. Leavenworth, KS.

[2]Ibid., 19

[3]Ibid., 29, 50, 80

[4]Ibid., 78

[5]Ibid., 82

[6]Ibid., 19

[7]"Occupation Forces in Europe Series, 1947-48, The Third Year of the Occupation Fourth Quarter, 1 April – 30 June 1948, Volume 1," Office of the Chief Historian, European Command, 1948:113, Combined Arms Research Library, Ft. Leavenworth, KS.

[8]"Occupation Forces in Europe Series, 1948, The Fourth Year of the Occupation, 1 July –31 December 1948, Volume 1," Office of the Chief Historian, European Command, July 1949:11, Combined Arms Research Library, Ft. Leavenworth, KS.

[9]Ibid:12

[10]Ibid., 13

[11]"Occupation Forces in Europe, The First Year, 1945-1946, Volume 1," Office of the Chief Historian, European Command, August 1947:169, Combined Arms Research Library, Ft. Leavenworth, KS.

[12]"Occupation Forces in Europe, The Second Year, 1946-1947, Volume 2," Office of the Chief Historian, European Command, August 1947:25, Combined Arms Research Library, Ft. Leavenworth, KS.

[13]"Occupation Forces in Europe Series, 1947-48, The Third Year of the Occupation, First Quarter, 1 July – 30 September 1947, Volume 1," Office of the Chief Historian, European Command, 1948:2, 3, 142, Combined Arms Research Library, Ft. Leavenworth, KS.

[14]"Occupation Forces in Europe Series, 1947-48, The Third Year of the Occupation, Third Quarter, 1 January – 31 March 1948, Volume 1," Office of the Chief Historian, European Command, 1948:26, Combined Arms Research Library, Ft. Leavenworth, KS.

[15]"Occupation Forces in Europe, The First Year, 1945-1946, Volume 1," Office of the Chief Historian, European Command, August 1947:105, Combined Arms Research Library, Ft. Leavenworth, KS.

[16]Ibid., 105, 202

[17]Ibid., 105, 107, 167

[18]"Occupation Forces in Europe, The Second Year, 1946-1947, Volume 1," Office of the Chief Historian, European Command, August 1947:100, Combined Arms Research Library, Ft. Leavenworth, KS.

[19]"Iraq," CIA World Factbook, https://www.cia.gov/cia/publications/factbook/geos/iz.html, 20 May 2007

[20]L. Paul Bremer and Malcolm McConnell, *My Year in Iraq: The Struggle to Build a Future of Hope* (New York: Simon and Schuester, 2006), 38

[21]Ibid., 4

[22]Ibid., 37

[23]Ibid., 87

[24]Ibid., 215, 394

[25]Ibid., 113

[26]"Occupation Forces in Europe, The First Year, 1945-1946, Volume 1," Office of the Chief Historian, European Command, August 1947:25, Combined Arms Research Library, Ft. Leavenworth, KS.

[27]Bremer, 17

[28]Ibid., 115-116

[29]Ibid., 123, 172, 173

[30]Cordesman, XX-XIII, 15

[31]Ibid., 257

[32]Ibid., XXV

[33]Bremer, 39-40

[34]Cordesman, 152

[35]Ibid., 256

[36]Ibid., 257

CHAPTER 4

INFORMATIONAL MEANS

Informational comparison will be possible as public information was given its own chapter in the occupation journals. The journals mention information sources to include radio and the policies that govern their use. Consideration must be given for the speed in which information traveled in the 1940s. Dissemination of information was considerably slower than now due to the technology of the time.

Control of the populous was very important at the conclusion of World War II in order to minimize the problems with governing the United States Sector. The allied forces did not want to lose control of the gains that had been made at such a high cost. Some of the control measures used were emplacement of curfews, confiscation of all weapons, the restriction of entertainment (radios were only allowed for information and no music was played), no postal or telephone use, travel by foot or bicycle only, railroads only for military use. Only doctors, nurses, and clergy were allowed the use of motor transport.[1]

This seems to be a direct contradiction to the situation in Iraq. The only similarity between the two seems to be the use of the curfew to control the movement of the populous. The retention of motor vehicles has led to the creation and use of the Vehicle Borne Improvised Explosive Device (VBIED). Cell phones, working phone service, and internet also permitted the insurgents to coordinate their forces.

Ambassador Bremer does mention that he used television on a weekly basis for a broadcast directed at the Iraqi people to inform them of the coalition vision for the nation and the coalition actions.[2] This was a successful use of information to influence the people but it was also a two edged sword. In Germany, radio stations, until they were controlled and censored by the military, continued to broadcast propaganda. This was seen with the seizing of the Flensburg Radio Station at the beginning of the German occupation.[3] In Iraq, radical clerics have enormous amounts of freedom in their preaching to the people in Iraq. Al Jezeera fuels this and continues on its inflammatory rhetoric even today.

Generating good will with the German people was very important to the American leaders in Germany. Part of this program was a series of Christmas amnesties announced by the OMGUS. On 24 December 1946, General Joseph McNarney made his first address to the German people. During his address, he granted amnesty to approximately 800,000 Nazi followers. These citizens had not profited from Nazi greed nor were they major offenders.[4] General Lucius Clay repeated this policy on 15 December 1947 when he granted a Christmas Amnesty to approximately 2,000 German prisoners.[5]

Use of the Press in Germany

The issue of bad press, generated by the allied nation's news agencies against the Americans, began to appear in 1946. To counter this General McNarney instituted regular monthly press interviews in addition to General Clay's biweekly press conferences. General McNarney would regularly remind his staff of the importance of a good relationship and proper attitude towards correspondents.[6]

As a part of the relaxing of limitations on the German populous, OMGUS granted German newspapers and German press the right to request interviews with military government officials. The first press conference they were allowed to attend was in Berlin on 21 February 1947, almost two years after then end of the war.[7] The press was permitted to discuss German political problems and allowed to make comments in German newspapers on matters of policy of the occupying powers. However, it was illegal for German political parties or the press to spread militaristic or antidemocratic ideas or rumors aimed at disrupting Allied unity.[8]

Fraternization Policy in Germany

Another difference seen between the two plans was the implementation of a fraternization policy. This policy initially stated that Soldiers were only allowed to converse with "very young children" the authority to talk to adults was not added until later.[9] This is a marked difference in Iraq where the average Soldier is encouraged to talk and interact with everyone in the society. Ambassador Bremer mentions numerous times in his books where he would go to a committee meeting of various factions and converse with all of them, women included.

The non-fraternization policy implemented in Germany was to prevent the German people from influencing the American soldiers. Military leaders feared that, without the policy, it would create unfavorable public opinion in America.[10] The policy also protected the German people. Citizens who fraternized were subject to assault by other Germans; also, handbills and posters would be circulated criticizing German women for associating with American soldiers.

During the first year of the occupation, the restrictions on the fraternization policy began to be lifted. Soldiers were authorized to talk to children on 8 June 1945, in open places with Germans on 10 July 1945, and all restrictions were lifted by 1 October 1945.

By 1 July 1947, Germans citizens were permitted to attend United States Army motion picture theaters, except for those in restricted areas.[11] With no insurgent threats appearing in Germany, almost all restrictions on where German nationals could travel were lifted. By 10 June 1948, American members of clubs and messes were authorized to bring Germans and displaced persons as guests. Passes required to attend snack bars and clubs were eliminated.[12]

Censorship in Germany

The military immediately imposed censorship on all civilian communications. Under the control of the G2 and G5 Divisions of the Supreme Headquarters, this was to control information and for intelligence use.[13] There were four phases to the censorship. First, all communications were prohibited, all mail impounded, and message services were suspended. In the next phase, reopening of communications facilities for use in Germany only occurred. International communication was to be done only through prisoner of war, civilian internee, or Red Cross messages. The third phase relaxed the restrictions on communications in Germany and allowed limited international communications. The final phase had only limited restrictions on internal and external communications.[14]

Postal routes reopened within the United States zone of Germany in October 1945. Contact with individuals living outside of the American zone would come later. This was only to be used among the civilian population as the United States military had their own postal services. In December of 1945, authorization for interned German Soldiers to communicate through the mail with displaced persons in the occupied area.

41

As mentioned above in the third phase, international postal service was restarted 1 April 1946.[15]

Telephone service was slow to reestablish with the first intra city lines coming into operation in Frankfurt by June 1945. Intra zonal phone service became operational in February 1946. Establishment of telegraph service was relatively faster than the phone service and became operational in November 1945, but international authorization was delayed due to disagreements among the allied powers.[16]

German Youth Activities

One of the questions during the early days of the occupation was what to do with all of the children. OMGUS took a step in the summer of 1945, when it established youth offices to provide institutional care for orphaned, needy, or delinquent youths. The next step was to provide for those who still had families and on 7 July 1945, a letter was issued by the Supreme Commander authorizing religious organizations to conduct welfare and athletic activities for young people.[17] These initial programs grew into large and larger efforts to improve the activities to help rehabilitate the German youths.[18]

The youth programs established were for both boys and girls. Efforts were made to recruit competent female volunteers to operate the programs.[19] The establishments of the youth programs were not one-time affairs. Regular conferences were held in Frankfurt to discuss problems with funding, lack of athletic equipment, and lack of qualified personnel. These efforts paid off when summer camps for displaced children were opened on 16 June 1947. Eventually thirty-two camps were operational accommodating 22,000 children. In order to insure the health of the children, each child received 3,000 calories of food a day.[20] This is far in excess of what the average German was receiving.

Occupation forces were also encouraged to donate funds for the entertainment of children at Christmas time. Through the youth programs and donations from Soldiers, 60 percent of the displaced children numbering 47,000 youths and 20 percent of German children were entertained at 1946 Christmas parties.[21] The program had been so successful that during Christmas of 1947 1,118,817 children were entertained, by this time only 68,787 were children of displaced persons.[22] These programs went far to generate good will for the American forces in Germany.

Use of the Press in Iraq

With the increased speed of telecommunications since 1945, the use of the press has changed greatly. Whereas in 1945 weeks could pass before pictures would be seen in America, today movies made on cell phones are in the news in days if not hours. The support received by the military and officials working in Iraq from the press is much different than what was received in Germany. Ambassador Bremer states his frustration with the press, "Over the summer I had visited many reconstruction projects, but they got little press coverage. These stories apparently weren't as attractive to editors and producers as looting, power outages, gasoline lines – and eventually the mounting violence."[23]

The rigid controls that were enacted in 1945 over the radio, press, and newspapers did not occur in Iraq. In Germany, the press was granted the right to publish the news as long as it did not spread militaristic or antidemocratic ideas or rumors. The press could be shutdown or the reporters jailed if they did so. In Iraq, Muqtada al-Sadr had published a vitriolic attack on Iraqi's cooperating with the coalition and had listed 124 persons by name. By 1 August 2003, at least one person had been shot to death.[24]

The fact that the coalition and world press continue reporting attention-getting news as long as they focused on the insurgent attacks and ignored optimistic stories. Terrorists will continue to pick high profile targets in order to use attacks as "weapons of mass media." They will also continue to manipulate United States official briefings with planted questions. Insurgents also use our own media resources against America by using information operations to exploit, exaggerate, and falsify coalition attacks that have caused civilian casualties and any negative publicity anti-Arab or Islamic statements.[25]

There have been cases of the positive use of the press in Iraq such as when, "the coalition TV station announced the Brothers deaths, celebratory gunfire had broken out in all of Iraq's major cities."[26] The brothers identified were Saddam's sons Uday and Qusay. Another example was Saddam Hussein's capture and the televised trial. By publicly announcing these events and through the weekly broadcast by Ambassador Bremer and the military leaders in Iraq, the belief was that positive public opinion would sway towards the coalition forces.

Olympic Readmittance

Another powerful tool that Ambassador Bremer exploited was the opportunity to readmit Iraq to the Olympics. The intention was to have Iraq attend the Olympic Games in one year, 2004. To make this happen would go far to showing to the world the new Iraq and would hopefully increase the patriotism and nationalism for Iraq. Through much hard work, Iraq was reaccepted into the Olympics after the election of the Iraqi Olympic committee.[27] Unfortunately, the participation of Iraq in the 2004 Olympics did not seem to have much effect on the solidarity of the Iraqi nation.

The use of the press, media (television, radio, and internet), and successful information operations campaign greatly affects the policies and strategies devised and utilized during the occupations of Iraq and Germany. In Germany, direct hands on control of information and use of youth programs assisted in the decrease of anti-Allied acts. This was not so in Iraq. As OIF was declared a "liberation" versus an "occupation" the direct control seen in Germany was impossible. This has led to a number of differing groups, Al Qaeda and Muqtada Al-Sadr to name a few, to use various information resources to their benefit and the detriment of the United States.

---

[1]"Occupation Forces in Europe, The First Year, 1945-1946, Volume 1," Office of the Chief Historian, European Command, August 1947:24-25, Combined Arms Research Library, Ft. Leavenworth, KS.

[2]L. Paul Bremer and Malcolm McConnell, *My Year in Iraq: The Struggle to Build a Future of Hope* (New York: Simon and Schuester, 2006), 136

[3]"Occupation Forces in Europe, The First Year, 1945-1946, Volume 1," Office of the Chief Historian, European Command, August 1947:18-19, Combined Arms Research Library, Ft. Leavenworth, KS.

[4]"Occupation Forces in Europe, The Second Year, 1946-1947, Volume 1," Office of the Chief Historian, European Command, August 1947:47, Combined Arms Research Library, Ft. Leavenworth, KS.

[5]"Occupation Forces in Europe Series, 1947-48, The Third Year of the Occupation, Second Quarter, 1 October – 31 December 1947, Volume 1," Office of the Chief Historian, European Command, 1948:52, Combined Arms Research Library, Ft. Leavenworth, KS.

[6]"Occupation Forces in Europe, The Second Year, 1946-1947, Volume 2," Office of the Chief Historian, European Command, August 1947:22, Combined Arms Research Library, Ft. Leavenworth, KS.

[7]Ibid., 36

[8]"Occupation Forces in Europe Series, 1947-48, The Third Year of the Occupation, Second Quarter, 1 October – 31 December 1947, Volume 1," Office of the Chief Historian, European Command, 1948:3, Combined Arms Research Library, Ft. Leavenworth, KS.

[9]"Occupation Forces in Europe, The First Year, 1945-1946, Volume 1," Office of the Chief Historian, European Command, August 1947:75, Combined Arms Research Library, Ft. Leavenworth, KS.

[10]"Occupation Forces in Europe, The First Year, 1945-1946, Volume 2" Office of the Chief Historian, European Command, August 1947:83, Combined Arms Research Library, Ft. Leavenworth, KS.

[11]"Occupation Forces in Europe Series, 1947-48, The Third Year of the Occupation, First Quarter, 1 July – 30 September 1947, Volume 1," Office of the Chief Historian, European Command, 1948:26, Combined Arms Research Library, Ft. Leavenworth, KS.

[12]"Occupation Forces in Europe Series, 1947-48, The Third Year of the Occupation, Fourth Quarter, 1 April – 30 June 1948, Volume 1," Office of the Chief Historian, European Command, 1948:83, Combined Arms Research Library, Ft. Leavenworth, KS.

[13]"Occupation Forces in Europe, The First Year, 1945-1946, Volume 3" Office of the Chief Historian, European Command, August 1947:96-97, Combined Arms Research Library, Ft. Leavenworth, KS.

[14]"Occupation Forces in Europe, The First Year, 1945-1946, Volume 2" Office of the Chief Historian, European Command, August 1947:152, Combined Arms Research Library, Ft. Leavenworth, KS.

[15]Ibid., 154

[16]Ibid., 155

[17]"Occupation Forces in Europe, The First Year, 1945-1946, Volume 3" ," Office of the Chief Historian, European Command, August 1947:13:14, Combined Arms Research Library, Ft. Leavenworth, KS.

[18]"Occupation Forces in Europe, The Second Year, 1946-1947, Volume 1," Office of the Chief Historian, European Command, August 1947:95, Combined Arms Research Library, Ft. Leavenworth, KS.

[19]"Occupation Forces in Europe Series, 1947-48, The Third Year of the Occupation, First Quarter, 1 July – 30 September 1947, Volume 2," Office of the Chief Historian, European Command, 1948:97, Combined Arms Research Library, Ft. Leavenworth, KS.

[20]"Occupation Forces in Europe, The Second Year, 1946-1947, Volume 1" ," Office of the Chief Historian, European Command, August 1947:11, 80, Combined Arms Research Library, Ft. Leavenworth, KS.

[21]Ibid., 47

[22]"Occupation Forces in Europe Series, 1947-48, The Third Year of the Occupation, Second Quarter, 1 October – 31 December 1947, Volume 1" Office of the Chief Historian, European Command, 1948:52, Combined Arms Research Library, Ft. Leavenworth, KS.

[23]Bremer, 113

[24]Ibid., 121-122

[25]Anthony H. Cordesman and Patrick Baetjer, *Iraq Security Forces: A Strategy for Success* (Westport, CT: Preager Security International, 2006), 35, 36, 39

[26]Bremer, 119

[27]Ibid., 118, 307

CHAPTER 5

MILITARY MEANS

The United States Military in Germany

The American army had begun planning for the occupation of Germany three years before the end of the war even before the invasion of Normandy. This time allowed the Allied Forces to begin to train the required civil affairs and administration personnel to administer to the conquered areas as soon as liberation occurred. The name of the occupation plan of Germany was entitled Eclipse. The plan was to have an Army type garrison force strong enough to occupy, meet tactical needs, provide security against subversive actions, and give logistical support to the military government. The initial estimates had the garrison force requirements at 400,000 Soldiers.[1]

The Forces

The initial forces involved in the garrisoning of the United States occupied areas of Germany were the 6th, 12th, and 21st Army Groups consisting of sixty-one combat divisions: forty-two Infantry Divisions, four Airborne Divisions, and fifteen Armored Divisions, plus naval task forces, and with Air Force elements present.[2]

The Army forces were eventually pared down to the 6th and 12th Army Groups consisting of ten Divisions in three Corps. The reduction of forces, in Germany, was expected to occur over time but was actually begun immediately. By July of 1945, a major reduction and redistribution of forces to America and the Pacific Theaters had taken place.[3] This is very similar to the reduction in forces that occurred after the cessation of hostilities with Iraq.

The American planners had realized early on that there was a different type of force required for the garrisoning of Germany. A combat force was not what was needed: a police type occupation force was necessary. This was due to Washington denying the troop request for additional assets, as the war in the Pacific Theater was still ongoing. This occupation force was to total 363,000 troops; 144,000 in seven divisions, 78,000 in the Air Force, and 116,000 in headquarters and service units.[4] These forces were divided into the Eastern and Western Military Districts in Germany; these numbers do not include the garrison forces in Austria or the Allied forces in other sectors.

The Army had begun the occupation with the belief that there would be a likelihood of general armed uprising. This ended up not being the case, the only significant resistance encountered in 1945 and the beginning of 1946 was individual acts of indiscipline, sabotage, and general crime.[5] This lack of an insurgency led the Army to believe that further reductions in troop strength were in order. Troop occupation numbers began to rapidly fall from November 1945 on.

Troop strength dropped to 281,000 in November 1945, with four divisions being reformed into a new organization, the constabulary, numbering 38,000 Soldiers. Three divisions were to remain as the mobile reserve in case of problems that the local police or constabulary could not handle. These divisions were reorganized to be mobile cavalry style forces, which could rapidly respond to any situation in the American Zone and Austria.[6]

By 1 July 1946 the occupation and garrisoning of Germany was in full swing and few problems had been encountered that required a dedicated combat force so the decision was made to reduce troop strength even further. The European Theater was to total 329,601 troops, 14,504 of which were in Austria and 48,287 in the Air Force. The number of forces continued to reduce even further so that by 1 July 1947 the number of troops in the European Theater numbered only 117,000. General Clay, the theater commander, wished to reduce the Air Force contingent from 40,000 airmen to 8,500 by 1 June 1948. He believed that they were an administrative burden and that he did not have a need for them except for air transportation and communications.[7]

Security remained a large concern for the forces in the European Theater. Even though a large partisan campaign had not appeared, tensions with the former ally Russia were continuing to grow. In the first half of 1947, over 33 percent of the forces in the theater were being used for security. This totaled approximately 33,000 Soldiers.[8] By 31 December 1947, the troop numbers for the theater had dropped even further to 121,839 troops. To compensate for the loss of these forces, the Army employed 492,571 indigenous workers.[9] Troop strength finally dropped to an all time low of 113,689 for the European Theater in June 1948.[10]

To help solve some of the personnel shortfall issues, inquiries were made, in March 1947, into recruiting for and forming a foreign legion to assist in guarding Germany. Initial analysis suggested that this type of organization could replace as much as 20 percent of the American forces within a year. At this time, 'Polish Guard Companies" did exist. These were private security organizations made up of non-Germans. Evidence had proven that the discipline in these units was lax and that their involvement in black marketing and other crimes were common. General Clay quashed this concept by replying that the Army could not run an American occupation with mercenaries.[11] In order to support the long duration occupation that was to occur, technical, leadership, and continuous training schools were establish, where possible, from the very beginning.[12]

The Constabulary and German Police

General Eisenhower announced the structure of the constabulary at the end of October 1945. They were to consist of high caliber personnel with an efficient communications network, the most modern weapons, and have sufficient vehicles and liaison aircraft to make it mobile.[13] The unit was to be a highly trained, motivated, and mobile police force that was to be supported by the remainder of the Army. It consisted only of American Soldiers, as the inclusion of foreign troops would have had to overcome varying language and training barriers that existed.[14]

The organization of the occupation was along geographic lines to coincide with the German Civil Administration. The organization was to consist of one constabulary headquarters with three brigade headquarters. In order to prepare the Soldiers for their duties a school was established in Sonthofen, Germany. They were to not only be proficient in their military duties but they were trained to know police methods, how to make arrests, and how to deal with foreign populations.[15]

Activation of the constabulary occurred on 1 July 1946, with a personnel strength of 33,076 officers and men. Its duties also involved the responsibility for border control at fifteen crossing points, involving roads and rails, with patrols beginning almost immediately upon their inception.[16] Not only were the constabulary forces immediately involved in patrols but they also saw action. On 7 July 1946, the 26th Constabulary Squadron investigated the alleged assault of a German farmer and his sister by Soviet troops, in the American zone, near Nentschau. When they arrived, Soviet forces fired upon them, the Americans returned fire and one Russian Soldier was killed in the exchange.[17]

On 15 March 1947, the border patrol mission was reassigned to OMGUS and the border police placed under their control.[18] The drawdown of forces occurring throughout the theater also affected the constabulary. In January 1948, they were reorganized with 1,236 Officers, 94 Warrant Officers, and 18,876 Soldiers; totaling 20,206 men.[19] This reorganization required the deactivation of a number of units.

The plan for re-establishment of local police forces was crucial for the Americans to help control the insurgency that they believed would occur after the occupation. Reorganization of the local police forces occurred on 7 July 1945, after being de-Nazified. From June 1945 until the beginning of 1946, the local police forces increased in strength from 12,000 to 24,500 members. This was achieved through the creation and operation of twenty basic training schools in Germany, which allowed the Americans to turn out a great number of police officers in a short time.[20]

On 6 November 1945 the Allied Control Commission, consisting of all of the allied nations in Germany, came to the agreement that the German police would be armed to deal with crime. This was due to the successful De-Nazification that was taking place.[21] Their authority grew even further when they were granted the right, on 8 August 1947, to make arrests as long as those arrests did not deal with war crimes or security.[22]

The Insurgency

At the time of the surrender of Germany, the plans for an insurgency had been in the formative stage. The swift arrest of key SS, SD, and Gestapo troops and leaders had deprived a potential resistance of key leadership. This led to the early months of the occupation with the most serious threats being disorderly displaced persons and German youths causing mayhem. Disbandment of German forces went smoothly and according to plan after 8 May 1945. Operations focused on two key tasks: liquidation of command functions and a gradual release of the German POWs in American hands of which there were 7.2 million.[23]

By the fall of 1945, the Army determined that they would not face a strong resistance movement as had been feared. This was due to level of destruction that the war had caused to the infrastructure and the people, which resulted in war weariness for many. In addition, the number of forces deployed by the United States and the other nations in their zones were overwhelming. The Werewolf Organization, which had been touted as a last resort resistance movement, turned out to exist only as a propaganda tool and no active resistance materialized.[24] Only two serious incidents were reported during the beginning of the occupation.

On the evening of 19 October 1946, a bomb detonated on the windowsill of the de-Nazification office at Backnang, fifteen miles northeast of Stuttgart. Two more bombs exploded later that night. One, at the local military police station and the second at the de-Nazification bureau in Stuttgart. No injuries were reported as the bombs were set to detonated during the evening. On 27 October 1946, a second incident occurred when a bomb exploded on the window ledge of the switchboard for the Spruchkammer. No injuries were reported as a result of this attack as the bomb detonated during the night. The apprehension of an ex-SS Major with fourteen others occurred in November. The SS Major was hung and ten of the others went to prison.[25]

Signs of subversive activity did exist but they were uncoordinated and showed no signs of large scale planning. Groups of disgruntled youths would appear and annoy the occupying authorities, threaten German women who associated with Americans, and deal with the black market. The first signs of actual sabotage and unrest reared their head in October 1945. Petty sabotage consisting of wire cutting, a wall smearing campaign against women associating with Americans was observed along with anti-Semitic feelings. During this time, a slight increase in assaults on American personnel arose.[26] This seems to be based more on a sense of frustration than a Nazi resurgence. The withdrawal of American troops saw a rise in the number of incidents occurring. In order to overcome this rising tide of lawlessness, the local police began to be armed and the constabulary was formed. Roving patrols by the local units also helped to increase the security.[27]

In the occupation of Germany all weapons from the populous were confiscated or turned in immediately. Some of the items taken consisted of shotguns, pistols, and other hunting weapons, including explosives. Punishment for violators included death and imprisonment. To insure that caches or stockpiles did not exist, large-scale search operations occurred in July and November 1945. Searches continued on a smaller scale with continuously fewer items found.[28]

Another step taken to minimize the chance for an insurgency to arise were specific policies to insure public safety. Among these policies were a curfew, travel restrictions, ban on certain articles, exclusion from military areas, and prohibition of meetings, parades, and public assemblies. Another step taken was strict border control established at the very beginning of the occupation. It was realized that this was a sure

54

method of maintaining law and order. On 30 March 1946, a lifting of the zone wide curfew occurred. Unannounced checks and searches and the establishment of roadblocks would still be utilized to maintain control.[29]

Once the insurgency did not arise, pilferage and petty crime became the new enemy. In December 1945 over $2 million in pilferage of military items was reported.[30] This was reduced to $869,000 in April of 1946 and to $414,000 by June of that same year. The main reason this was occurring was due to the lack of adequate security. In addition to the steps taken above, new directives aimed at controlling the displaced persons were put into affect in January and March of 1946. These directives helped to decrease the crime and losses experienced.[31]

Crime was organized into three different categories. First was juvenile delinquency. This type of crime was traditionally unorganized. First time offenders were turned over to their parents or welfare workers. Second time offenders had the parents held responsible for the crime. This quickly eradicated this type of crime. Social programs established by the army also helped to dissuade the juveniles.[32]

The second type of crime was black market operations which were, in part, fueled by the pilferage that was taking place. This type of crime had far-reaching impact. With the civilian population using the black market, devaluation of the mark and undermining of the economy took place. These illegal operations also offered subsistence to subversive groups. To overcome this employment of food and clothing rationing, and price control enacted by the civil administration took place. To further dissuade violators, the trial of these crimes happened in the military courts.[33]

The third type of crime was the depredation on the displaced persons in Germany. These displaced personnel were not just Jewish refugees but also other foreign nationals who had been shipped to Germany during the war or trapped here by the initiation of it. The estimations were that by 8 May 1945 there were over 2,320,000 displaced persons in the American zone.[34]

The crimes against the displaced persons grew as they rampaged after liberation and the conditions of the camps grew worse. To help manage these crimes, control measures were put in place utilizing security guards, raids by military police looking for contraband, and establishment of roadblocks to recover stolen vehicles.[35] One final step taken was on 2 September 1947; Headquarters, European Command, announced a limitation on meetings, demonstrations, parades, or other gatherings outside of established assembly areas by displaced persons.[36]

Displaced persons also committed many of these crimes. On 30 July 1947, two American Soldiers were attacked and captured by a number of Jewish displaced persons. The capture of the Soldiers was due to frustrations over the situation in Germany and the conditions of the displaced persons camps. Counter Intelligence Division members and other Soldiers later rescued them.[37]

Foreign Influences: The Soviet Impact

As tensions with the Soviet Union grew so did the number of incidents involving them. Contact was still maintained by the military leaders of each of the zones through the Allied Control Council and this was the forum where protests would be raised. On 20 December 1947, General Clay cited a number of incidents in which Soviets in military uniforms apprehended or attempted to apprehend German civilians in the American zone.[38]

In the fall of 1947, a visitor from the Soviet sector attempted to instigate labor strikes in the cities of Bremen, Kassel, and Stuttgart. They were to protest the bad food situation and the inefficiency of German public agencies. In December, strikes took place all over the American zone, but conducted in an orderly manner.[39] Additional strikes occurred in May 1948, which involved 25,000 to 40,000 people. They were protesting the same issues as during the protests in December.[40]

A number of espionage incidents were reported beginning in 1947. With the discovery of fourteen suspected Soviet agents in October, eight in November, and thirteen in December. During this same period, twelve cases of suspected sabotage were reported, but who conducted them or their level of effectiveness was unknown.[41] This included the discovery of additional agents in 1948 and on 9 November 1948, the arrest of twenty persons on suspicions of espionage occurred. It was later determined that they were spying on behalf of Czechoslovakia.[42] During this same time the Polish consulate and Polish Red Cross were caught conducting espionage, had their accreditations cancelled, and were expelled from the American zone.[43]

The United States Military in Iraq

The speed in which the invasion of Iraq took place shocked not only the American and Coalition forces, but also the world. The build up of forces in the Middle East progressed much faster than in the first Gulf War in 1991. As opposed to the policy in World War II, the military did not expect to conduct nation building in Iraq at the completion of OIF. The discussion and implementation for a long-term occupation force was unplanned for at any levels of the military leadership or civilian government. Another fallacy that existed was the expectation that once the invasion took place the soldiers and civil servants would remain in place and continue to administer to and protect the country. This did not happen.

Before the invasion, the RAND Group did a study of seven previous occupations and determined that a force of 500,000 troops would be required for the occupation of Iraq. A successful occupation traditionally allocates 20 Soldiers per 1000 civilians. In May of 2003, the United States had only approximately 130,000 troops in Iraq.[44]

The Forces

The plan for the occupation of Iraq differs significantly from that of the occupation of Germany. Whereas in Germany the civilian and military plans were for the United States to be there for the long haul, this was not the case in Iraq. There are some indications that the original plan called for a rapid drawdown to 30,000 Soldiers who were not identified to conduct stability operations. The United States and Coalition forces believed that they would inherit stability, not be forced to create it. Based on this assumption, the American Forces did not plan for the long-term occupation requiring extensive civil-military operations, the need for large numbers of Military Police, nor human intelligence (HUMINT) resources.[45]

There are strong indications of a disconnect between the civilian administration and military leaders, in that U.S. Central Command (CENTCOM) war plans called for robust stability operations and much larger force levels than the administration chose to deploy.[46] As the state of Iraq came more to light with its degraded infrastructure, lack of police, military, and civil servants, the decision to increase the force numbers took place. The Chief of Staff of the Army made the decision, in conjunction with his advisors.

The original decision was to maintain a force level of approximately 138,000 troops at least until the end of 2005. As the breakdown in society and the insurgency grew, American plans changed and begin a troop increase to 160,000 after the 15 December 2005 elections. During this time, General Peter Schoomaker declared that over 100,000 troops made need to remain in Iraq into 2009.[47]

This would become increasingly difficult as the force levels of the United States Army in 1945 and 2003 varied widely. World War II had mobilized large numbers of the American work force for the duration of the conflict plus six months. This made not only active duty forces available but National Guard and Reserve units also. This was much different from the selected mobilization of those Reserve and National Guard assets that has occurred in Operation Iraqi Freedom (OIF). With units conducting a yearly, or less, rotation, units at the end of their cycle become less aggressive. The units tend to conduct fewer patrols and combat operations.[48]

One of the military factors that differ between the occupation of Germany and the liberation of Iraq is the existence and freedom of action of the individual militia groups. Disarmament and disbandment of Military and Paramilitary forces took place immediately, upon the occupation of Germany in 1945, with the United States Army as the only armed force authorized.[49] This is different in Iraq with each tribe or group allowed to have an armed militia and to police their respective areas.

For much of the first year of the occupation, there was more talk and political maneuvering conducted than actual substantive action about disarming Iraqi civilians and

Iraq's Sh'ite and Kurdish militias. Ambassador Bremer believed that, "Iraq's long-term stability required that all military forces be under central government control."[50] Disarmament of the militias was only begun in force in February 2004, five months before the disbandment of the CPA and recognition of the Iraqi Governing Council. The disarmament agreement covered nine major militia groups, which numbered approximately 100,000 former resistance fighters.[51]

There were three approaches to the disarmament of the militia groups. First, qualified militia members would be recruited into officially recognized Iraqi Security Forces (ISF). Secondly, retiring the unqualified members with government supplied veteran's benefits. Lastly, reintegrate others into Iraq's civil society and economy through education, training, or job placement.[52]

The ability to integrate the former resistance fighters into the ISF would have given the military a good start on its formation. This plan changed when the initial two battalions which were to be completed was increased to twenty-seven within the same year timeline by Secretary Rumsfeld.[53] The ongoing de-Ba'athification process did not help the creation of the military either. De-Ba'athification blocked the Americans from developing the military, security, and police forces from recruiting many of the most experienced leaders and military personnel for much of the first year of the occupation.[54]

The 1st Marine Division added to the problems by appointing a former Republican Guard General to command the "Fallujah Brigade." This was done without clearance or guidance from the Pentagon or the CPA.[55] This appointment, of the former Republican Guard General, went against the policy of de-Ba'athification while it was occurring. This unilateral action set back the training and deployment of that force and

60

politically weakened the American position in the eyes of the Iraqi people. It also shows the disconnect between the military plan and the civilian plan.

From June to December 2004, the Defense Department reported that the ISF totaled approximately 219,000 personnel. This includes 7,000 in the armed forces, 36,000 Iraqi Civil Defense Corps (ICDC) members, 84,000 police officers, 18,000 border enforcement staff, and 74,000 Facilities Protection Service (FPS) personnel.[56] The majority of these personnel were not adequately trained, armed, motivated, or led. The failure of the Iraqi National Guard (ING) Battalions participating in the battle of Fallujah in 2004 highlights this. General John Abizaid recognized the problem and stated that more old army officers needed incorporation into the ING despite de-Ba'athification.[57]

The Coalition forces originally accepted the cost for training and equipping these forces with the United States assuming the majority of the requirement until the economy of Iraq could be restarted. By May 2005, spending reached $5.8 billion for military, security and police forces while an additional $5.7 billion was requested from Congress to accelerate their development. In 2004, the budget for the Iraqi military and police was $450 million with an additional $1 billion devoted to additional security measures.[58]

Not all interactions with the militias went well. A militia organized under the control of Muqtada Al Sadr, the son of a famous cleric killed by Saddam Hussein's forces in the 1980's, and based in Sadr city, is one such example. Al Sadr's militia, named the Mahdi Army, remainder a threat to peace and stability and they proved this on 10 October 2003 when they attacked a patrol of the 2nd Armored Cavalry Regiment. The attackers consisted of over 300 fighters who were well armed. [59] The patrol eventually drove the attackers back and later that week the Mahdi Army forces stood down and the situation began to diffuse.

The Iraqi Police

When the invasion and occupation of Iraq occurred, the local police forces also disbursed along with the military and governmental officials. Rioting, looting, and crime ran rampant through out all of Iraq. The American civilian and military leaders had not expected nor prepared to handle this level of anarchy. As the Americans took control, only 4,000 poorly trained police were reporting for duty.[60]

Ambassador Bremer believed that with the achievement of peace and safety, the local Iraqi police officers would feel safe to leave their families and return to work. This is important, as more order would reduce the crime that was happening on every street corner. The looters and criminals were extremely well armed with assault rifles, machine guns, and rocket propelled grenades (RPG). He hoped to achieve this when he requested additional aid from the military and General Abizaid stated that he could provide 4,000 additional military policemen to help keep the peace.[61]

This plan was successful as by mid-July 2004 over 15,000 police officers had returned to duty across the country. By August 2004 estimates, place the number of available police at 65,000-75,000. This number was inaccurate as only 32,000 could be verified. Ambassador Bremer initially authorized the spending of $120 million on training and equipping the police forces.[62] The numbers vary so radically due to the loss of records during the invasion, police chiefs listing members that do not exist to pocket the funds, and the ongoing de-Ba'athification process. Just as teachers, military officers, and civil servants, to be a police officer had required one to also belong to the Ba'ath party.

Estimates placed the number of required police forces in Iraq at 40,000 members. Due to the deteriorated infrastructure and the inadequate facilities, expectations were that it would take six years to train this number of personnel in Iraq and would cost $750 million in the first year alone. In order to speed up the process, the decision was made by the CPA to look outside Iraq. The best choice was the Taszar airbase in Hungary which could accommodate 16,000 officer candidates a year.[63]

Due to a political impasse, Hungary decided to not host the police academy and the CPA realized the need to utilize the second alternative, Jordan. Jordan agreed to provide the facilities and visas to train 1500 police candidates a month but the first class could not begin until November 2004.[64] Even though the facilities were closer and eased transportation burdens, the training base was not fully adequate for the CPAs needs. Due to the limited amounts of housing facilities, a shortening of training to meet the deadline of 40,000 police officers was required. In addition, the range facilities could not handle rifles or fully automatic weapons, leaving cadets to train with only pistols and a few shotguns.

In order to renovate these facilities in Jordan and additional training facilities in Iraq, the allocation of over $190 million was required. This money was well spent as the police-training program in Jordan involved 322 instructors from sixteen countries and, by December 2005, with over 32,000 police cadets trained successfully. Problems with the selection process occurred as no set criteria was established or enforced. On more than one occasion, unsuitable candidates arrived at the academy and were rejected for medical, age or political reasons.[65]

The Insurgency

Reports by the Defense Intelligence Agency (DIA) and Multi-National Force – Iraq (MNF-I) show that the number of serious violent incidents climbed from none in May 2003 to over 200 in June and then increased sharply from there to an average of 1,500 monthly through February 2005. In July 2004, administration spokesmen were reporting that the manning of the initial insurgency totaled a 5,000 strong core force mostly composed of Former Regime Loyalists (FRL), but the experts on the ground believed that number was closer to 12,000-16,000.[66] Of that 12,000-16,000, General Abizaid believed that the 5,000 hard core Ba'athist were the greatest threat.[67]

The insurgency as it developed utilized many different tactics and techniques to good affect against the Coalition forces. From September 2003 to October 2004, there was a balance between the types of attacks utilized from VBIEDs, to IEDs, direct fire, and indirect fire.[68] Even the threat of surface to air missiles (SAMs) appeared, delaying the reopening of the Baghdad International Airport to commercial services in 2003.[69]

On 7 August 2003, the first use of a VBIED was reported. Its use was against the Jordanian embassy in Baghdad. The intelligence reports state that the Mukhabarat, local secret intelligence cells, were responsible not foreign fighters.[70] This was about to change and the VBIED was to become very popular for all insurgent forces. VBIEDs utilize a minimum amount of effort and resources for the significant affect they generate.

Two VBIED incidents that took place greatly affected the situation in Iraq. The first was on 17 May 2004 when the Iraqi Governing Council President, Izzadin Salim, was assassinated utilizing this method. The second was the bombing of the United Nations Headquarters on 19 August 2003, which later caused the UN to scale back their operations in Iraq.[71]

Another tactic which is popular is the kidnapping or killing of foreign envoys, women, and foreign workers who help to legitimize the Iraqi government. The aim of these attacks is to influence nongovernmental organizations (NGOs) from assisting and participating in the rebuilding of Iraq. These tactics help to influence foreign nations but these same tactics can be used to influence domestic policy when the target is Iraqi teachers and journalists.[72]

In Germany in 1945, all personal weapons were confiscated and turned into military government, this is not so in Iraq. The establishment and operation of the militias and the inability to seal the national borders create problems with trying to control the flow of weapons. A cultural issue also exists where, as a symbol of manhood, a man was allowed to retain a fully automatic rifle. This has left a large cache of available weapons for the insurgency to use against the Coalition forces.

In Germany, unless a prisoner of war was guilty of war crimes, their release came quickly after the cessation of hostilities. By May 1945, prisoners who had had careers as farmers, coal miners, transport workers, and in other key industries began to be released to help rebuild the country's infrastructure.[73] Much the same occurred in Iraq, unless identification of a man as a war criminal, security risk, or a foreigner, he was released back to society. Unfortunately, the difference is that the majority of Iraqi prisoners had few skills that were applicable to the rebuilding of the country.

In the beginning of the occupation, the facilities to hold the detainees were barely adequate and usually located in the same facilities where prior abuses occurred under Saddam's regime. Until the creation of a proper system, the release process was difficult and time consuming. There was a requirement to identify those responsible for war crimes or who were security threats.[74] A central database was difficult to establish as many personnel records were destroyed, missing, or inaccurate.

In order to stem the rise of the insurgency, American and Iraqi forces increased the number of arrests made to assist in whittling down the pool of insurgents. Major General William H. Brandenburg, commander of U.S. detention operations in Iraq, stated that the coalition forces were arresting on average 50 suspected insurgents a day with the 2005 daily average approaching 70 people. In January 2005, the American forces had approximately 7,900 detainees in captivity. By May 2005, this had risen to 11,350.[75]

Foreign Influences: Iran and Saudi Arabia

The influence that Iran and Saudi Arabia have had during the occupation of Iraq cannot be overlooked. Due to the size of the Iraqi border and the small size of forces available for border security infiltration by state sponsored and non-state sponsored actors exists. Insurgent forces and supplies have been reportedly smuggled over the Iraqi border, from a number of different nations, to help fuel the growing insurgency in Iraq. This has dramatically increased the threat that exists in Iraq.

These actions have historical significance, such as in the Iraq and Iran war of the 1980s, and are future oriented. Both Saudi Arabia and Iran have a stake in the future of Iraq. Saudi Arabia, predominantly Sunni, does not wish to see a strong Shia nation on their border who would have strong religious ties with Iran, who is predominantly Shia.

This potential for Iran and Iraq to form an alliance has significant impact culturally, militarily, and economically for the entire region.

Iran has similar interest in not wishing for a strong Sunni state to be on their border for the same reasons as Saudi Arabia. This has cause Iraq to become a battleground that may affect the Middle East for a number of years to come. Iran would also like to make the final claim that they have won the Iran-Iraq War, even though the war has been over since 1988 and it had ended in a stalemate.

The success of the American Military in German is directly proportional to their ability to adjust to the new situation they were facing in the post-World War II environment. The creation and use of the constabulary, successful de-Nazification of the police forces, and the knowledge that the military would remain in Europe for the long haul set the conditions for a successful occupation. In Iraq, delays in the creation of the Iraqi National Guard and in the United States Army transformation have significantly affected the suppression of the insurgency.

---

[1]"Occupation Forces in Europe, The First Year, 1945-1946, Volume 1," Office of the Chief Historian, European Command, August 1947:48, 52, 53, Combined Arms Research Library, Ft. Leavenworth, KS.

[2]Ibid., 41

[3]Ibid., 58-59

[4]Ibid., 122, 142

[5]Ibid., 142

[6]Ibid., 143

[7]"Occupation Forces in Europe, The Second Year, 1946-1947, Volume 1," Office of the Chief Historian, European Command, August 1947:6, 58, Combined Arms Research Library, Ft. Leavenworth, KS.

[8]"Occupation Forces in Europe Series, 1947-48, The Third Year of the Occupation, First Quarter, 1 July – 30 September 1947, Volume 1," Office of the Chief Historian, European Command, 1948:3, Combined Arms Research Library, Ft. Leavenworth, KS.

[9]"Occupation Forces in Europe Series, 1947-48, The Third Year of the Occupation, Second Quarter, 1 October – 31 December 1947, Volume 1," Office of the Chief Historian, European Command, 1948:23-24, Combined Arms Research Library, Ft. Leavenworth, KS.

[10]"Occupation Forces in Europe Series, 1947-48, The Third Year of the Occupation Fourth Quarter, 1 April – 30 June 1948, Volume 1," Office of the Chief Historian, European Command, 1948:61, Combined Arms Research Library, Ft. Leavenworth, KS.

[11]"Occupation Forces in Europe, The Second Year, 1946-1947, Volume 1," Office of the Chief Historian, European Command, August 1947:59, Combined Arms Research Library, Ft. Leavenworth, KS.

[12]"Occupation Forces in Europe, The First Year, 1945-1946, Volume 3," Office of the Chief Historian, European Command, August 1947:28, Combined Arms Research Library, Ft. Leavenworth, KS.

[13]Ibid., 19

[14]"Occupation Forces in Europe, The First Year, 1945-1946, Volume 1," Office of the Chief Historian, European Command, August 1947:123, 127, Combined Arms Research Library, Ft. Leavenworth, KS.

[15]"Occupation Forces in Europe, The First Year, 1945-1946, Volume 3," Office of the Chief Historian, European Command, August 1947:20, 25, Combined Arms Research Library, Ft. Leavenworth, KS.

[16]"Occupation Forces in Europe, The First Year, 1945-1946, Volume 1," Office of the Chief Historian, European Command, August 1947:199-200, Combined Arms Research Library, Ft. Leavenworth, KS.

[17]"Occupation Forces in Europe, The Second Year, 1946-1947, Volume 1," Office of the Chief Historian, European Command, August 1947:3, 4, Combined Arms Research Library, Ft. Leavenworth, KS.

[18]Ibid., 69

[19]"Occupation Forces in Europe Series, 1947-48, The Third Year of the Occupation, Third Quarter, 1 January – 31 March 1948, Volume 1," Office of the Chief Historian, European Command., 1948:90, Combined Arms Research Library, Ft. Leavenworth, KS.

[20]"Occupation Forces in Europe, The First Year, 1945-1946, Volume 2," Office of the Chief Historian, European Command, August 1947:160-162, Combined Arms Research Library, Ft. Leavenworth, KS.

[21]Ibid., 163

[22]"Occupation Forces in Europe Series, 1947-48, The Third Year of the Occupation, First Quarter, 1 July – 30 September 1947, Volume 1," Office of the Chief Historian, European Command, 1948:9, Combined Arms Research Library, Ft. Leavenworth, KS.

[23]"Occupation Forces in Europe, The First Year, 1945-1946, Volume 1," Office of the Chief Historian, European Command, August 1947:61, 62, 63, 121, Combined Arms Research Library, Ft. Leavenworth, KS.

[24]"Occupation Forces in Europe, The First Year, 1945-1946, Volume 2," Office of the Chief Historian, European Command, August 1947:141, Combined Arms Research Library, Ft. Leavenworth, KS.

[25] "Occupation Forces in Europe, The Second Year, 1946-1947, Volume 1," Office of the Chief Historian, European Command, August 1947:37-38, Combined Arms Research Library, Ft. Leavenworth, KS.

[26]"Occupation Forces in Europe, The First Year, 1945-1946, Volume 2," Office of the Chief Historian, European Command, August 1947:141-142, Combined Arms Research Library, Ft. Leavenworth, KS.

[27]Ibid., 141-142

[28]Ibid., 127

[29]Ibid., 136, 137, 165

[30]Ibid., 136-137

[31]"Occupation Forces in Europe, The First Year, 1945-1946, Volume 3," Office of the Chief Historian, European Command, August 1947:64, 165, Combined Arms Research Library, Ft. Leavenworth, KS.

[32]"Occupation Forces in Europe, The First Year, 1945-1946, Volume 2," Office of the Chief Historian, European Command, August 1947:165-166, Combined Arms Research Library, Ft. Leavenworth, KS.

[33]Ibid., 166

[34]"Occupation Forces in Europe, The First Year, 1945-1946, Volume 3," Office of the Chief Historian, European Command, August 1947:158, Combined Arms Research Library, Ft. Leavenworth, KS.

[35]"Occupation Forces in Europe, The First Year, 1945-1946, Volume 2," Office of the Chief Historian, European Command, August 1947:167, Combined Arms Research Library, Ft. Leavenworth, KS.

[36]"Occupation Forces in Europe Series, 1947-48, The Third Year of the Occupation, First Quarter, 1 July – 30 September 1947, Volume 1," Office of the Chief Historian, European Command, 1948:48, Combined Arms Research Library, Ft. Leavenworth, KS.

[37]Ibid., 47

[38]"Occupation Forces in Europe Series, 1947-48, The Third Year of the Occupation, Second Quarter, 1 October – 31 December 1947, Volume 1," Office of the Chief Historian, European Command, 1948:59-60, Combined Arms Research Library, Ft. Leavenworth, KS.

[39]Ibid., 60-61

[40]"Occupation Forces in Europe Series, 1947-48, The Third Year of the Occupation Fourth Quarter, 1 April – 30 June 1948, Volume 2," Office of the Chief Historian, European Command, 1948:41, Combined Arms Research Library, Ft. Leavenworth, KS.

[41]"Occupation Forces in Europe Series, 1947-48, The Third Year of the Occupation, Second Quarter, 1 October – 31 December 1947, Volume 2," Office of the Chief Historian, European Command, 1948:62, Combined Arms Research Library, Ft. Leavenworth, KS.

[42]"Occupation Forces in Europe Series, 1948, The Fourth Year of the Occupation, 1 July – 31 December 1948, Volume 1," Office of the Chief Historian, European Command, July 1949:98, Combined Arms Research Library, Ft. Leavenworth, KS.

[43]"Occupation Forces in Europe Series, 1948, The Fourth Year of the Occupation, 1 July – 31 December 1948, Volume 2," Office of the Chief Historian, European Command, July 1949:59-60, Combined Arms Research Library, Ft. Leavenworth, KS.

[44]L. Paul Bremer and Malcolm McConnell, *My Year in Iraq: The Struggle to Build a Future of Hope* (New York: Simon and Schuester, 2006), 10

[45]Anthony H. Cordesman and Patrick Baetjer, *Iraq Security Forces: A Strategy for Success* (Westport, CT: Preager Security International, 2006), 17

[46]Ibid., 1

[47]Ibid., 53, 321

[48]Bremer, 314

[49]"Occupation Forces in Europe, The First Year, 1945-1946, Volume 1," Office of the Chief Historian, European Command, August 1947:64-65, Combined Arms Research Library, Ft. Leavenworth, KS.

[50]Bremer, 244

[51]Cordesman, 87-88

[52]Ibid., 87

[53]Bremer, 150

[54]Cordesman, 14

[55]Bremer, 344-345

[56]Cordesman, 67

[57]Bremer, 338

[58]Cordesman, 1, 74

[59]Bremer, 190-191

[60]Ibid., 19

[61]Ibid., 19, 32

[62]Ibid., 128

[63]Ibid., 128-129

[64]Ibid., 152, 168

[65]Cordesman, 111, 217

[66]Ibid., 30, 61

[67]Bremer, 235

[68]Cordesman, 31

[69]Bremer, 117

[70]Ibid., 126-127

[71]Ibid., 359

[72]Cordesman, 37, 40

[73]"Occupation Forces in Europe, The First Year, 1945-1946, Volume 1," Office of the Chief Historian, European Command, August 1947:63-64, Combined Arms Research Library, Ft. Leavenworth, KS.

[74]Bremer, 133

[75]Cordesman, 200

CHAPTER 6

ECONOMIC MEANS

Economic Situation in Germany

By June of 1945, the German economy had reached its lowest point; industrial production was at less than 2 percent capacity. This was due to wartime damage and lack of import of required resources, there was no existing trade between the various allied zones. Through the rebuilding efforts of the Americans, the release of prisoners of war (POW) for use in crucial industries, and reprioritization of resources, the end of 1945 saw the industrial capacity rise to 10 percent of the existing capacity. These efforts were prioritized into key areas that focused on sustaining life in the occupied areas through the coming winter. Some of the industries focused on were agriculture, railways, reestablishment of electrical power, reestablishment of inland water transport, and production of brown coal for heating.[1]

With the oncoming winter, three projects were vital: food, housing, and coal. Coal was critical for industry, rail transportation, and heating of homes, offices, and factories. Unfortunately, the coal found in the American zone was of poor quality. Called brown coal it could only be used for heating and small industries. The Army was forced to prioritize and disburse the available coal to the civilian population. The problem that existed and faced the Americans was that the war had badly damaged the German coal industry and the Wehrmacht had drafted all of the able body coal workers. With the industry damaged or destroyed, returning workers had little incentive to return to work and were short food and equipment.[2]

In order to overcome these problems, the Army took steps to increase the food ration for the miners; 3,600 calories per day for those above ground and 4,000 calories per day for those below ground. In addition, the transportation of available coal and mining equipment was given priority after redeployment and troop maintenance. Due to the lack of rail and road assets, inland waterways on the Danube and Rhine rivers were the preferred method of moving the coal. This method of transportation was utilized once the labor service companies had repaired the canals. The barges were eventually able to move 230,000 tons per month of coal.[3]

The fall and winter of 1945 were hard on the German people as they had had little time to rebuild and repair after the cessation of hostilities and before the winter came. This problem with survival remained in the fall of 1946 when the United States Army provided 31 truck companies, consisting of over 3,000 trucks, to move potatoes. The movement of firewood also occurred in this manner. This project, named Operation SPUD, was also assisted by twenty percent of the civilian trucks from forty-six communities and lasted from 31 October 1946 until 1 January 1947.[4]

Some of the economic programs instituted with the occupation of Germany, in order to aid in controlling the populous and to stabilize the economy, was the closure of all financial institutions except for savings banks. The populace was ordered to exchange their Germany currency for military currency; this also included all foreign currency. Failure to do so was punishable by any penalty short of death. All foreign assets, to include bank accounts, bank checks, drafts, bills of exchange, or other methods of payment, were to be reported to the government and only the military government could authorize foreign monetary transactions.[5] The introduction of scrip currency, introduced by the OMGUS on 14 September 1946, had over $83,000,000 in German money exchanged between the government and the populous.[6]

Currency control was required for a number of reasons, the most important being the active black market which dealt in all types of commodities.[7] An unchecked black market could destabilize all of the efforts undertaken in the American zone. A byproduct of this was the banning of the use of cigarettes as a form of currency. This ban became effective on 9 June 1947. The only authorized importation of cigarettes was to be through the PX system.[8] The second reason was to track the population and attempt to find any Nazi party members that had disappeared into the country when the war ended.

Zonal Economic Cooperation

During the Potsdam Conference of 17 July 1945, the attending allied leaders agreed to certain economic principles. Among these was the decision, that the primary concern was reestablishment of agriculture and the peaceful domestic industries. In addition, war materials were not to be produced and Germany was to become a single economic unit among all four zones.[9]

As part of the rebuilding of Germany based on agreements made between the allied nations America focused on five key steps for rebuilding in their zone. First, excess industrial capacity was to be removed and shipped to other nations as reparations. This was to be concentrated on industries that could be used for wartime manufacturing. Secondly, the German economy was to be decentralized to eliminate excessive concentrations of power, such as cartels. Prior to World War II, cartels were endemic to the German economic system. Thirdly, those industries, which remained that could be utilized for war making capabilities, such as chemicals and vehicle manufacturing, were to be rigidly controlled. Fourth, all aircraft manufacturing was to be prohibited. Finally, all power generation was to be strictly controlled by the military government.[10]

The first step taken in the merging of the various economic systems was an agreement made between the British and American zones on 3 December 1946. The goal was to merge the two zones economically and make them self sufficient within three years.[11] The success of the British and Americans would lead the French agreeing to coordinate their economic policy in the matters of foreign and interzonal trade, customs, and freedom of movement for people and goods by February 1948.[12]

As the British and the American zones continued to become more integrated, the need to centralize finance was identified and in March 1948, a central bank for the two zones was established in Frankfurt.[13] The establishment of a central bank would lead to the first trizonal endeavor when the French zone integrated their bank into the central bank in Frankfurt on 1 April 1948.[14]

Food Rationing

Due to the deprivations of war and the devastated nature of the economy, most German civilians at the end of the war were at a starvation level of food. There were reports that even the animals in the Berlin zoo had been slaughtered for their meat in the final days of the Third Reich. As the Americans began to consolidate their hold, in June 1945, the average German was subsisting on approximately 900 calories per day. This caloric intake rose to 1,550 calories per day and European procured rations began to augment the foodstuffs imported from America beginning in January 1946.[15] For fiscal year 1947 to 1948, to maintain the caloric intake of 1,550 calories for the German people, over $283,500,000 worth of food, fertilizers, seeds, and petroleum was shipped to

Germany from the United States and Western Europe. The amounts totaled over 1,750,000 tons of food alone.[16]

To help restart the agricultural market, nitrates from captured German munitions were released to the farmers for use as fertilizer. Excess American munitions were also demilitarized and given to the Germans, as this was cheaper than maintaining them or shipping them back to the United States. This also included trucks and other equipment, which were released by the Americans when the equipment was demilitarized.[17]

Labor Service Companies

After the end of World War II in Europe, large numbers of German soldiers were in allied forces' POW camps not only in Europe but also in the United States. In Germany those POWs that were not skilled in the critical industries needed to restart the country, worked in labor service companies. There were three types of labor service companies: civilian guard companies, technical labor service companies, and common labor service companies.[18]

By August of 1945, over 2,430 companies existed and were doing repair work all over the American zone until their eventual release. They repaired roads, housing, canals, and worked on other projects that required unskilled manual labor.[19] The amount of service companies were reduced in number as the release of POWs occurred. On 31 December 1945, there were only 2,058 companies and by 1 March 1946, only 1,100 still existed.[20]

Much as prisoners are treated in civilian jails in America, POWs were paid for the work that they preformed. On 23 December 1945, the daily rate for labor was established as 80 cents. Payment was dispersed by the military government to the dependents of former POWs or the POWs themselves. The rate of exchange was made at thirty cents to the mark versus the going rate of ten cents to the mark to help revitalize the economy quicker. In all, 80,080,000 marks were paid of for labor conducted during internment. [21]

Cost of Occupation

Prior to the enactment of the Marshall Plan in 1948, the rebuilding of Germany was being undertaken with wartime funds. In July 1946, Secretary of State James F. Byrnes had attended the Paris Peace conference that was attended by all of the allied nations. During the conference, the American stance was that General Joseph T. McNarney, as the governor of the American sector, would receive orders to cooperate with all powers in the realms of finance, transportation, communications, trade, and industry. This was to hopefully curtail the costs of the occupation as the Americans were paying $200,000,000 a year for the occupation of Germany. The bulk of this funding was being spent on food for the German people.[22]

Following this direction from Secretary Byrne, General McNarney proposed to the Allied Control Council on 20 July 1946 that the Americans would join any other nation in the formation of a single economic unit. Only the British were interested as the French and Russian representatives responded with criticism. As a result, on 9 August 1946 the British and Americans reached an agreement on the broad principles of economic unity between the two zones.[23]

Marshall Plan

The Marshall Plan was originally called the European Recovery Program (ERP). President Truman requested funding for the ERP in his Presidential farewell address on

19 December 1947. The plan, as requested, was to originally cost $17 billion.[24] The Economic Recovery Act was eventually passed in 1948, which included the Marshall plan. The Senate vote, led by Senator Arthur Vandenburg, was 69-17 and in the House, it was 329-74.[25] The ERP initially authorized the expenditure of $5,300,000,000 during the first year.[26] $3.5 million of these funds were allocated on 12 July 1948 for the purchase of railcars to be utilized in improving the economy and transportation of vital supplies in the zone.[27] As a majority of Army assets were still being used to assist the German people.

The plan for Germany was to have them self-sufficient as soon as possible. From 1948 to 1949 the bizonal area received over $1,100,000,000, intended to make them self supporting by 1952.[28] The majority of this funding was to go to supporting the population of Europe with the necessities of life. These necessities totaled into the millions for food and industry. Food procurement totaled $69 million by 10 August 1948 and industry received $31 million for vehicles, resources, and supplies to rebuild the infrastructure.[29]

In order to rehabilitate the entire economy of Europe, the maximum amounts of resources that purchasable in Europe would be done. Milk from Denmark, security guards from Poland and other nations, truck drivers from France are a few of the ways funds were routed into the rebuilding of Europe. By 10 September 1948, the amounts of funds being spent had increased dramatically, food procurement for the year totaled $84 million and industry totaled $66 million.[30]

Just assigning funds and buying food for the German people was not enough. The ERP was helping to get the German people back on their feet as a viable, productive member of Europe and not as beggar. Before the war, Germany had contributed to the economic stability of the remainder of Europe by being a large exporter of produced goods. In 1947, Germany was only able to export a total of $275 million. Through an active recovery plan, this was to be increased to $1.8 billion by 1951.[31]

The overall recovery of Germany was to cost the American taxpayers $3.2 billion from 1946 to 1952. $1.6 billion was financial aid prior to the Marshall Plan, from 1946 to 1948 and $1.6 billion under the Marshall Plan, which lasted from 1948 to 1952. In 1953, the amount was valued at $3 billion, $2 billion was in grants and $1 billion was eventually repaid to the United States. These grants were an important feature of the Marshall Plan to help create a Cold war bastion against the anticipated aggression of the Soviet Union.[32]

The Economic Situation in Iraq

There were large differences between the economies of Germany and Iraq. Germany had had a diverse industrial base with a large middle class and private sector. This was not the case with Iraq, the one crucial industry, oil, was state owned and operated. The enforced socialism of the Iraq state had destroyed the middle class private sector through lack of options and stagnation.[33]

In 1945, the United States had had more than three years to prepare for the post war occupation of Germany. On the other hand, the United States military did not plan nor expect to conduct an occupation and governing of Iraq at the completion of OIF. Expectations had also existed that the Iraqi Army personnel and civil servants would remain at their jobs, act as a stabilizing force, and not desert which lead to the social upheaval that occurred.[34] Cordesman stated that the Bush administration failed to develop and budget for anything approaching a meaningful aid program.[35]

A basic fact realized early in the occupation of Germany was that with the infrastructure damaged as severely as it was, basic industries need to be restarted as soon as possible. A number of factories from the Ford plant at Cologne, to sawmills and thread mills became the immediate priorities. The fear of starvation, lack of housing, and inadequate clothing motivated the military government to direct all available resources to their rebuilding and production. Luxury industries soon began again but were subject to labor and resource requisitioning for other necessary industries.[36]

This plan is very similar to the sewer, water, electricity, and trash (SWET) programs that have been enacted in Iraq. In the neighborhoods where these programs have been enacted and worked, crime statistics, insurgency attacks, and protests occur at lesser degrees. It is recognized that those who work have less time or inclination to join the insurgency. This was also a tactic utilized in Germany where those who did not have jobs were put into work gangs that provided manpower for the rebuilding efforts or necessary industries.

Ambassador Bremer saw the necessity of programs such as SWET as he toured one of the few textile factories that remain after the liberation of Iraq. The factory was outdated, in poor repair, and making articles of clothing that no one wished to own due to the social mismanagement and lack of investment brought on by Saddams reign. He states that, "We faced a crisis as serious as the one America experienced in the Great Depression."[37] This is after he has seen the state of many of the industries in Iraq, primarily the oil industry. Equipment was outdated, the company's were mismanaged, and were in debt.

The CPA identified electricity as a vital requirement for the rebuilding of Iraq. Electricity is critical for industry and normal everyday operations for those living in the cities of Iraq. An initial evaluation of the electrical grid of Iraq in 2003 showed that only 300 megawatts being generated in the entire country. Security for the power lines were also an issue as Iraq had almost 12,000 miles of power lines and they were vulnerable to looting and sabotage. The strategic program for the reconstruction of the electrical grid was on track by 2 October 2004 with power generation having reached 4,217 megawatts.[38]

As the oil industry was the only industry in Iraq that had the possibility of quickly being rehabilitated to be able to provide export funds, attention and funds were quickly routed its way. This was because the primary facility at Daura had been built by American oil interests in 1955, but had not been upgraded since. In mid-June 2003 after the establishment of the CPA, the Pentagon shifted responsibility for rehabilitation of the oil facilities from CJTF-7 to the CPA. This transfer of responsibility did not include the transfer of funds, which delayed the rehabilitation until funds were allocated by Congress or released by the United Nations.[39]

Another problem that Ambassador Bremer continued to encounter was sabotage of the pipelines, which caused a sharp decline in anticipated oil-export earnings. The security problem was hindered by the over 4,000 miles of pipeline requiring protection.[40] Despite the security issues, 2003 saw $5.1 billion in exported oil with an increase to $17 billion in 2004. The year 2005 started out well with an initial oil exportation of $6.2 billion in the first four months.[41]

Ambassador Bremer reports a problem that had been solved with the forced use of military currency, devaluation. Due to the lack of confidence in the Dinar and rampant inflation, the Iraq economy was on the verge of collapse due to mismanagement under Saddam. This caused more problems by trying to shore the economy up than to start over with new money. Some of the problems that Iraq would have faced by converting to a new money system would have been the international acceptance of the funds and the linkage of their economy into whatever nation's currency they adopted.

As the CPA began its evaluation of the different sectors of the Iraq economy, it was found that the financial system was bankrupt. Saddam had made the banks make loans available to his allies on very favorable terms. This caused the banks to operate on political versus economic guidelines. This led to mass inflation of the Dinar due to a lack of confidence. As a result, Saddam would print more money to overcome the inflation. This tended to be a temporary situation, as he would continue to do so every time the need arose.[42]

The CPA decided to overcome this problem by developing a Dinar exchange program and printing new Dinars. Once the new Dinar began circulation, it became very successful and was to strengthen by 30 percent versus the dollar, in a relatively short time. In order to assist in the strengthening of the Dinar, the Baghdad Stock Exchange reopened on 24 June 2004, with record shares traded. Another way the Dinar was strengthened and the economy was stimulated was by paying civil servants in the new

Dinar and purchasing local products versus the use of subsidies which existed under Saddams rule.[43]

Before the beginning of the war, unemployment had been at 50 percent. To overcome this, the CPA began public works programs such as the rebuilding of the irrigation canals connecting the Tigris and Euphrates rivers in the Shia south. This created over 100,000 jobs and cleared close to 20,000 kilometers of canals. This project helped to engender respect towards the coalition of the moderate Shi'ites.[44] The success of these projects is show in estimations as of 2005, which place the unemployment rate at twenty-five to thirty percent.[45]

Cost of Occupation

The rebuilding of Iraq was going to take time and money. In order to do this without expending all of the resources that America had, requests for independent groups to conduct assessments of the cost of rebuilding. The initial estimate of the World Bank stated that $50-75 billion would be required for reconstruction in the areas of power generation, agriculture, manufacturing, and other sectors. In April 2004, the American Congress appropriated approximately $2.5 billion for the initial recovery of Iraq, but it was determined that that money would be spent by mid-August.[46]

Initially Ambassador Bremer had requested from President Bush an increase of the $2.5 billion already given by Congress to $5 billion. The $5 billion was based on estimates made by Ambassador Bremer's staff and the World Bank. In August 2004, the World Bank realized that the state of Iraq was worse and that the immediate funding needed was in the realm of $20 billion. This funding was for the necessities required to get Iraq back on its feet and to revive the oil production capacity after decades of neglect under Saddam. Congress eventually approved a supplemental reconstruction budget of $18.6 billion towards the end of the existence of the CPA.[47]

Some of the required capital could be offset by $277 million held by the United Nations (UN) in escrow under the "Oil for Food" program. Initially, the UN stalled on the disbursement of the funds. By 19 August 2004 the UN, who has to approve all of the contracts that utilize these funds, had only approved one of 2,500 contracts. This significantly delayed the implementation of the initial reconstruction projects.[48]

The major issue that existed between the implementation of projects and the spending of funds in Iraq versus Germany has to take into consideration the numerous religious and cultural groups that exist. One of the ways that Ambassador Bremer overcame this was to provide funds into different accounts to pay for projects in different areas. He mentioned that he had to earmark several hundred million dollars for projects in the Sunni provinces. He also endowed the Kirkuk Foundation with $50 million in matching funds for the Kurds.[49]

The spending of these funds became problematic. Due to rolling power cuts and lack of trust in the reliability of the system and the Americans, only $1 billion of $4.4 billion in aid money was spent by April of 2005. Only $261 million of the allocated $1.7 billion allocated to the petroleum sector was spent by this same time.[50] The other problem attached to the spending of the funds was the difficulty in transferring funds from one fund site to another.

The growing security concerns also affected how and where money was spent. In order to provide security that was needed, money was transferred form the Iraq Relief and Reconstruction Fund (IRRF) to varying security projects. In November 2003, $1.8

85

billion transferred to varying security projects. In October 2004, an additional $1.8 billion was transferred to shore up security concerns in Iraq from the IRRF.[51]

The successful reconstructions of Germany and Iraq are based on the judicious application of funds. As the United States Army was the lead agency in the rebuilding of Germany, they were able to coordinate military and economic means to quickly provide funds and manpower where it was needed. In Iraq, this coordination did not exist. The leadership and responsibilities were split between the Departments of Defense and State leading to disunity in command and purpose.

[1]"Occupation Forces in Europe, The First Year, 1945-1946, Volume 1" ," Office of the Chief Historian, European Command, August 1947: 111, 112, Combined Arms Research Library, Ft. Leavenworth, KS.

[2]"Occupation Forces in Europe, The First Year, 1945-1946, Volume 3," Office of the Chief Historian, European Command, August 1947:73-74, Combined Arms Research Library, Ft. Leavenworth, KS.

[3]Ibid., 74-75

[4]"Occupation Forces in Europe, The Second Year, 1946-1947, Volume 1," Office of the Chief Historian, European Command, August 1947:97-98, Combined Arms Research Library, Ft. Leavenworth, KS.

[5]"Occupation Forces in Europe, The First Year, 1945-1946, Volume 1," Office of the Chief Historian, European Command, August 1947:27-28, Combined Arms Research Library, Ft. Leavenworth, KS.

[6]"Occupation Forces in Europe, The Second Year, 1946-1947, Volume 1," Office of the Chief Historian, European Command, August 1947:24-25, Combined Arms Research Library, Ft. Leavenworth, KS.

[7]"Occupation Forces in Europe, The First Year, 1945-1946, Volume 2," Office of the Chief Historian, European Command, August 1947:116, Combined Arms Research Library, Ft. Leavenworth, KS.

[8]"Occupation Forces in Europe, The Second Year, 1946-1947, Volume 1," Office of the Chief Historian, European Command, August 1947:52-53, Combined Arms Research Library, Ft. Leavenworth, KS.

[9]"Occupation Forces in Europe, The First Year, 1945-1946, Volume 1," Office of the Chief Historian, European Command, August 1947:92, Combined Arms Research Library, Ft. Leavenworth, KS.

[10]"Occupation Forces in Europe, The First Year, 1945-1946, Volume 2," Office of the Chief Historian, European Command, August 1947:5-6, Combined Arms Research Library, Ft. Leavenworth, KS.

[11]"Occupation Forces in Europe, The First Year, 1945-1946, Volume 1," Office of the Chief Historian, European Command, August 1947:45, Combined Arms Research Library, Ft. Leavenworth, KS.

[12]"Occupation Forces in Europe Series, 1947-48, The Third Year of the Occupation, Third Quarter, 1 January – 31 March 1948, Volume 1," Office of the Chief Historian, European Command, 1948:15, Combined Arms Research Library, Ft. Leavenworth, KS.

[13]Ibid., 26

[14]"Occupation Forces in Europe Series, 1947-48, The Third Year of the Occupation, Fourth Quarter, 1 April – 30 June 1948, Volume 1," Office of the Chief Historian, European Command, 1948:11, Combined Arms Research Library, Ft. Leavenworth, KS.

[15]"Occupation Forces in Europe, The First Year, 1945-1946, Volume 1," Office of the Chief Historian, European Command, August 1947: 111, 112, Combined Arms Research Library, Ft. Leavenworth, KS.

[16]"Herbert Hoovers press release of The President's Economic Mission to Germany and Austria, Report #1, German Agriculture and Food Requirements," February 28, 1947:16

[17]"Occupation Forces in Europe, The Second Year, 1946-1947, Volume 1," Office of the Chief Historian, European Command, August 1947:98, Combined Arms Research Library, Ft. Leavenworth, KS.

[18]"Occupation Forces in Europe, The Second Year, 1946-1947, Volume 2," Office of the Chief Historian, European Command, August 1947:184, Combined Arms Research Library, Ft. Leavenworth, KS.

[19]"Occupation Forces in Europe, The First Year, 1945-1946, Volume 1," Office of the Chief Historian, European Command, August 1947: 146, Combined Arms Research Library, Ft. Leavenworth, KS.

[20]"Occupation Forces in Europe, The Second Year, 1946-1947, Volume 4," Office of the Chief Historian, European Command, August 1947:200, Combined Arms Research Library, Ft. Leavenworth, KS.

[21]"Occupation Forces in Europe, The Second Year, 1946-1947, Volume 1," Office of the Chief Historian, European Command, August 1947:46, Combined Arms Research Library, Ft. Leavenworth, KS.

[22]Ibid., 8

[23]Ibid., 8, 18

[24]"Occupation Forces in Europe Series, 1947-48, The Third Year of the Occupation, Third Quarter, 1 January – 31 March 1948, Volume 1," Office of the Chief Historian, European Command, 1948:9, Combined Arms Research Library, Ft. Leavenworth, KS.

[25]Reston, James, "Remembering the Valiant Men Who Helped Put the Marshall Plan Together," The Kansas City Star, May 27, 1987

[26]"Occupation Forces in Europe Series, 1947-48, The Third Year of the Occupation, Fourth Quarter, 1 April – 30 June 1948, Volume 1," Office of the Chief Historian, European Command, 1948:7, Combined Arms Research Library, Ft. Leavenworth, KS.

[27]"Occupation Forces in Europe Series, 1948, The Fourth Year of the Occupation, 1 July – 31 December 1948, Volume 1," Office of the Chief Historian, European Command, July 1949:25, Combined Arms Research Library, Ft. Leavenworth, KS.

[28]Ibid., 26

[29]"First Report for the Public Advisory Board of the Economic Cooperation Administration," Washington D.C., August 25, 1948

[30]Ibid

[31]"European Recovery and American Aid Report by the President's Committee on Foreign Aid (Part 3)" Washington D.C., November 1947

[32]"The Fiftieth Anniversary of the Marshall Plan in Retrospect and in Prospect," The Netherland Institute of International Relations, The Hague, 15-16 May 1997; 32

[33]L. Paul Bremer and Malcolm McConnell, *My Year in Iraq: The Struggle to Build a Future of Hope* (New York: Simon and Schuester, 2006), 38

[34]Ibid., 37

[35]Anthony H. Cordesman and Patrick Baetjer, *Iraq Security Forces: A Strategy for Success* (Westport, CT: Preager Security International, 2006), 18

[36] "Occupation Forces in Europe, The First Year, 1945-1946, Volume 1," Office of the Chief Historian, European Command, August 1947:30, Combined Arms Research Library, Ft. Leavenworth, KS.

[37] Bremer, 62, 63

[38] Ibid., 18, 112, 179

[39] Ibid., 110

[40] Ibid., 109

[41] Cordesman, 34

[42] Bremer, 65, 74

[43] Ibid., 68, 77, 278, 388

[44] Ibid., 68

[45] "Iraq," CIA World Factbook, https://www.cia.gov/cia/publications/factbook/geos/iz.html, 20 May 2007

[46] Bremer, 116, 117, 119

[47] Ibid., 125, 231

[48] Ibid., 139

[49] Ibid., 268, 386

[50] Cordesman, 34

[51] Ibid., 54, 96

CHAPTER 7

CONCLUSION

> It was unrepeatable because Marshall Plan money rebuilt something that had already existed. Rotterdam was rebuilt in Rotterdam, not elsewhere, said Mr. Kindleberger. There was already a layout of streets and water mains.[1]
>
> Ann Hughey, "The Lessons of the Marshall Plan"
>
> At the end of WWII, the United States and the other Allies had clearly defeated the countries we had occupied. But here,' I said,' we've defeated a hated regime, not a country.[2]
>
> L. Paul Bremer and Malcolm McConnell, *My Year in Iraq*

The occupation of Germany beginning in 1945 and in some ways continuing today is a situation much different from the liberation of Iraq beginning in 2003. The occupation of Germany was based on the defeat and dismantling of a system, Nazism, which threatened the entire world. The beginnings of World War II are easily be traced to the mistakes made by the victorious powers at the conclusion of World War I with the Treaty of Versailles. Much as the invasion of Iraq in 2003 can also be traced to the mistakes made by the coalition powers in 1991 at the conclusion of the first Gulf War.

The key differences between the two situations are linked to the preparedness of the military structure to endure an occupation of a hostile nation. In 1943, the allied powers had begun the planning for a long term garrisoning and occupation of Germany to ensure a repeat of World Wars I and II would never occur again. The threat imposed by the expanding Soviet Union, and the need to counter this future and greater threat, quickly overshadowed the desire to ensure peace would reign on the continent.

This is not the case with Iraq. At the conclusion of the first Gulf War, the coalition did not follow the Iraqi military back into Iraq. This was done for one reason. The coalition would not have survived politically. The strength of the coalition forces was the reason the first conflict against Saddam Hussein was successful. The collaboration of nations not just from the West or Europe, but the inclusion of Middle Eastern nations also was crucial. This gave the coalition forces legitimacy in the eyes of neutral nations. The goal for that first coalition was the liberation, in a true sense of the word, of Kuwait. Not an invasion of Iraq, a step few wished to take.

Iraq poses many of the same problems that encountered in Germany. Comparisons can easily be made between the damage done to the infrastructure of Germany due to bombings by the Army Air Corps and the neglect Saddam Hussein showed for repairs and upgrades to Iraq's infrastructure. Even the oil infrastructure, the one international money producing industry in Iraq, was ignored and left to fend for itself. The reliance on 1960's equipment that was continuously breaking down was crippling the industry.

Comparisons can also be made to the disparities in the social situation that existed. It is true that Saddam did incorporate some Nazi style techniques, such as his dealing with the minority populations in Iraq like the Kurds. His ability to use chemical weapons on the members of his nation, which he viewed as lesser beings, draws eerie parallels with the treatment of the Jewish, Roma, and homosexual populations in 1930s and 1940s Germany.

Based on the concept of DIME, the success of policies implemented can be determined if either plan was ultimately successful. The issue of de-Nazification versus

91

de-Ba'athification sets the tone for the entire restructuring of the government, military and ultimately society. The process of de-Nazification was not based on a set time, as in Iraq, but on the need for an orderly transition. The American leadership in Germany at the end of the war realized that those people who knew and understood the system in Germany, though mostly members of the Nazi party were the correct people to keep in their jobs until the nation stabilized.

The situation on the implementation of the government has similar issues. The need to transition from a fascist system in Germany in 1945 was by far easier than in Iraq. Before the rise of Adolph Hitler, Germany had practiced democracy for a number of years. Hitler's reign had also been relatively brief so that the German citizens of voting age could easily remember a time when they had an active voice in choosing their civilian leaders.

The Office of Military Government United States (OMGUS) also applied political and military pressure to insure that political deadlocks and indecisions would not occur. Steps taken insured that the new German government would follow rules set by the occupation powers. On more than one occasion, OMGUS threatened to take back the power and authority granted to the new German government if they made the wrong decision. As a check on these decisions, the allied ruling council had final say on all votes cast. In Germany, the amount of time taken was never the deciding factor. Getting the right form of government, no matter how long it took, was the desired end state.

In Iraq, the decision for the transfer of the government to the Iraqi's was time based not event based. When Ambassador Bremer officially relinquished authority from the CPA to the Iraqi provisional government, certain decisions and steps had still not occurred. The Iraq council was fractured along religious and tribal lines and many individuals had separate agendas. These leaders were more focused on gathering power and financial benefits for themselves and their families. The basis for many political appointments was nepotism this led to many unqualified people filling critical positions. Ambassador Bremer forced and cajoled the council to cooperate and even to arrive for votes. In Germany, if the leadership was unresponsive fear of removal of their limited autonomy was for cooperation.

Control of the press and use of censorship was widely used in Germany. Control of these sources of information insured that the United States controlled the information into and out of their zone. Not only was this crucial in keeping the peace by eliminating seditious messages from the radio and press, but also allowed for easy dissemination of Allied information to the populous. On at least one occasion, a radio station was shutdown when enemy propaganda was aired or printed.

It took a number of years before German reporters attended the press conferences given by the OMGUS. This did not mean that the Commanding General did not understand or use the press effectively. At least two radio announcements proclaimed to the German people on Christmas amnesties that were to occur. In addition, daily Allied news broadcasts made for the benefit of the people detailing key information on food rationing and locations of other services.

In Iraq, this is not the case concern with freedom of the right to free speech and open debate has become a problem that has haunted the American forces. Muqtada Al Sadr and other militant clerics have continued to use not only the Al Jezeera network but also any other available mediums to send out their anti West rhetoric. The fact that

American forces have allowed the continued operation of these media outlets, which regularly incite uprisings through coverage of interviews, broadcasting of executions, and dissemination of inflammatory fatwa's have continued to fan the flames of discontent.

This lack of control has allowed the insurgent forces an outlet for their propaganda that has been extremely successful. Few commanders have been confident or able to utilize these same resources to put forth the American viewpoint. As seen in the Vietnam War, loss of the media leads to a decline in public confidence and will in both the military and political realms. The American commander has been kinetically focused for so many years that understanding, adapting, and coping with the changes that this type of battle employs is difficult.

The United States Army in 1945 was much larger and different from the American Army of 2003. This was in part due to the view taken after the sneak attack at Pearl Harbor where the nation viewed itself at war and committed all of the resources necessary to prosecute the fight. Once the planning had begun in 1943 for the occupation of Germany the determination was that the standard Army formation would be unacceptable for the new role required. The standard line division configuration was wrong for the needs of the occupation mission. Therefore, the constabulary was formed.

The constabulary was a cross between a cavalry regiment and a police Special Weapons and Tactics (SWAT) Unit. There were to have the most modern equipment and be heavily armed yet mobile to deal with any threat necessary. Their personnel were also to be special trained, not only in infantry skills but also, limited police style skills. Other than the occasional patrol or search mission, they were billeted at the barracks for when they were truly needed. Due to the lack of resistance in Germany, they existed for only a few years until the regular garrisoning forces assumed those responsibilities.

This ability to shift rapidly the composition, function, and mission of the units in Germany reflects the mindset that was prevalent. The configuration of the Army of 2003 to 2005 was for the linear battlefield. Even though, Army transformation had begun the basic structure of the Division remained linear. Its basis was the Army of Excellence, which was prepared to fight a symmetric war against the Soviet Union in Europe.

The belief was that technology would overcome any of the issues with the deficiencies of the unit when fighting an insurgency. These issues were the lack of manpower to garrison and hold key terrain while simultaneously conducting combat operations and the lack of human intelligence assets (HUMINT). This has proven not to be the case. Boots on the ground cannot be replaced by machines when a presence by the Soldier is what is needed to quell the insurgent.

When discussing the constabulary, an actual unit of this type does not exist in Iraq. Each unit has been forced to train each of their personnel to assume this role. Transformation has been a part of this with Field Artillery units, for example, assuming Infantry style missions and reflagging to Military Police and Transportation units. This need for each unit to be a jack-of-all-trades has become a by-product of the insurgency being fought where there are no frontlines and no rear area. The need for all to understand basic Soldier skills has been reinforced by the losses the Combat Support and Combat Service Support units have suffered, and the battles they have won.

One large difference seen in Iraq, much as with the freedom given to the ruling council, is the rapid rebuilding of the Iraqi National Guard and Police. This rebuilding,

95

retraining, and trust are unprecedented. As most of the junior officers and Soldiers were the same individuals engaging the coalition forces during the invasion and even during the first Gulf War. The rapid clearing of these individual makes one pause when considering the proclaimed success of de-Ba'athification and the future problems that this may contain.

This was not the case in Germany in 1945; there the only armed military authorized was the American army. The German police were authorized to carry pistols by 1947 only so that they could deal with the armed criminal elements in the country. This was only allowed after a thorough de-Nazification took place and no problems were ever reported or occurred. The use of time to undertake an exacting and complete de-Nazification insured that the German military, when reconstituted, had virtually no possible contamination by Nazi elements. This has allowed Germany to be a vital ally for the West during the Cold War and on into the twenty-first century.

Economically, in Germany only one organization had the ability to disburse funds and supplies to the citizens of Germany. This was OMGUS. The United States Army, or their contracted representatives, were the only organizations that coordinated and safe guarded supplies and guaranteed that they arrived with out pilferage. This insured that the right supplies arrived in time to the right place.

Once the occupation of Germany had begun, only limited time existed to prepare the German populous with food and fuel for the winter that was coming. Mountains of war stocked food, blankets, and other supplies were issued to those in need. Food was purchased and shipped with minimum delays from North America and Western Europe.

Eventually trade deals were made with the French and British control zones for resources and goods to help stimulate the economy.

This freedom was crucial to the success of the rebuilding of Germany from 1945 to 1947. In 1948, this became even easier with the establishment of the Marshall Plan, which would double the amount of aid already spent. Military resources and Soldiers were also used to help with the harvesting of food and the transportation of the food to market or distribution areas. This ultimately did not cost the military any more out of the budget than regular usage would have cost.

The situation in Iraq is not so simple. As an occupation did not occur, a complete takeover of the economy and infrastructure did not happen. The policy has been to offer contracts to those businesses in Iraq to help create jobs and jump-start the economy. This had caused delays along with the availability of the funds to pay for the projects or services. The increases in insurgent attacks had caused the cost for security on some projects to consist of half of the budget.

These projects under the term SWET (sewer, water, electricity, and trash) were often constructed in sections of the nation that had never had those amenities. The constant supplying of fresh water and electricity had continued to plague the CPA and the Iraqi council. Even when a city or a town with received newly established power lines, that area might only have electricity for a few hours everyday.

For a nation to prosper in the modern day, the exporting of resources or goods is crucial for the success of the economy. Germany was prepared in that many of its factories were easily rebuilt or retooled to provide goods for the rest of Europe and America. The diversity of their products guaranteed that there would never be a glut on the market and that there was always a need for them. This made the reconstruction of the German economy much easier than the Iraqi economy.

The Iraqi economy is based on only one major export, oil. There are some other exports, sand for concrete manufacturing and limited agriculture to name a few. These industries were never the moneymaker that oil was. Even with the outmoded and outdated equipment at the refineries and the embargos, Iraq continued to make a profit from the oil fields.

The same problems that existed with funds for the rebuilding of the national infrastructure exist with the refurbishment of the oil industry. The lack of speed on the dispersal of the funds hindered operations from the beginning. In addition, experts on oil were not on the ground rapidly to conduct assessment on the requirements need for the rebuilding. This contributed to the delays experienced. Security of these sites also became critical as the insurgents began to target them.

Overall, the occupation of Germany was far more successful than the liberation of Iraq due to the planning that took place years before it was needed. This planning identified personnel that required training, the need for civil governmental structure once the Army moved on, and the proper assumption was that the process was not going to be short. The initial identification that over 400,000 Soldiers would be required for the occupation of Germany made the senior leadership realize that America was in Germany for the long haul. Goals were not established on timetables for de-Nazification or a new governmental structure they were established based on effects accomplished. The ability to disburse funds and to make the necessary decisions was maintained in Germany by experts that understood the situation and knew what needed to be done.

Too many decisions were made in Iraq based on political necessity versus an honest assessment of the tactical and strategic situation. The belief that the Iraqi people would welcome the coalition with open arms and immediately stop fighting among each other, as they had been doing for hundreds of years was a fallacy that no one in the military or civilian leadership corrected. This same way of looking at the problems in Iraq with a Western styled viewpoint continue to bear little fruit for the successful rebuilding and restructuring of Iraq. If the German occupation is not analyzed or studied in detail and the lessons learned not incorporated then the American leadership will continue to misunderstand the requirements for nation building in the future and they will fail.

---

[1]Ann Hughey, "The Lessons of the Marshall Plan," *New York Times,* 7 June 1987, 4.

[2]L. Paul Bremer and Malcolm McConnell, *My Year in Iraq: The Struggle to Build a Future of Hope* (New York: Simon and Schuester, 2006), 27.

BIBLIOGRAPHY

Archives
Combined Arms Research Library
Ft. Leavenworth, KS 66027-1352

Occupation Forces in Europe, The First Year, 1945-1946, Volume 1-3. Office of the
Chief Historian, European Command. August 1947, Combined Arms Research
Library, Ft. Leavenworth, KS.

Occupation Forces in Europe, The Second Year, 1946-1947, Volume 1-7. Office of the
Chief Historian, European Command. August 1947, Combined Arms Research
Library, Ft. Leavenworth, KS.

*Occupation Forces in Europe Series, 1947-48, The Third Year of the Occupation, First
Quarter, 1 July – 30 September 1947, Volume 1-5*. Office of the Chief Historian,
European Command. 1948, Combined Arms Research Library, Ft. Leavenworth,
KS.

*Occupation Forces in Europe Series, 1947-48, The Third Year of the Occupation, Second
Quarter, 1 October – 31 December 1947, Volume 1-5*. Office of the Chief
Historian, European Command, 1948, Combined Arms Research Library, Ft.
Leavenworth, KS.

*Occupation Forces in Europe Series, 1947-48, The Third Year of the Occupation, Third
Quarter, 1 January – 31 March 1948, Volume 1-5*. Office of the Chief Historian,
European Command, 1948, Combined Arms Research Library, Ft. Leavenworth,
KS.

*Occupation Forces in Europe Series, 1947-48, The Third Year of the Occupation, Fourth
Quarter, 1 April – 30 June 1948, Volume 1-5*. Office of the Chief Historian,
European Command, 1948, Combined Arms Research Library, Ft. Leavenworth,
KS.

*Occupation Forces in Europe Series, 1948, The Fourth Year of the Occupation, 1 July –
31 December 1948, Volume 1-5*. Office of the Chief Historian, European
Command, July 1949, Combined Arms Research Library, Ft. Leavenworth, KS.

Harry S. Truman Library
Independence, MO

The Fiftieth Anniversary of the Marshall Plan in Retrospect and in Prospect. The
Netherland Institute of International Relations, The Hague, 15-16 May 1997

The Gallup Poll Public Opinion 1935-1971. Random House, New York, 1972

First Report for the Public Advisory Board of the Economic Cooperation Administration. Washington D.C., July 16, 1948

First Report for the Public Advisory Board of the Economic Cooperation Administration. Washington D.C., August 25, 1948

First Report for the Public Advisory Board of the Economic Cooperation Administration. Washington D.C., September 22, 1948

The Harry S. Truman Encyclopedia. The G.K. Hall Presidential Encyclopedia Series

European Recovery and American Aid Report by the President's Committee on Foreign Aid (Part 3). Washington D.C., November 1947.

Second Report to Congress of the Economic Cooperation Administration for the Quarter Ended September 30, 1948

Second Report to Congress of the Economic Cooperation Administration for the Quarter Ended December 31, 1948

Hughey, Ann. *The Lessons of the Marshall Plan.* New York Times, June 7, 1987

Reston, James. *Remembering the Valiant Men Who Helped Put the Marshall Plan Together.* The Kansas City Star, May 27, 1987

Draft, The President's Economic Mission to Germany and Austria, Report #3, March 1947, of 950B, Truman Papers

Herbert Hoovers press release of The President's Economic Mission to Germany and Austria, Report #1, German Agriculture and Food Requirements; February 28, 1947

Kindleberger to John C. deWilde, August 14, 1946; Memoranda, 1946; State Department File, Charles D. Kindleberger Papers

Kindleberger to Galbraith, April 24, 1948; Memoranda, 1946; State Department File, Charles D. Kindleberger Papers

Books

Bacevich, Andrew. *The New American Militarism.* Oxford University Press, New York, 2005.

Bremer, L. Paul, and McConnell Malcolm. *My Year in Iraq: The Struggle to Build a Future of Hope.* Simon and Schuster, New York, 2006.

Cordesman, Andrew H. and Baetjer, Patrick. *Iraq Security Forces: A Strategy for Success.* Praeger Security International, Westport, CT: 2006.

Iraq, CIA World Factbook. Available from https://www.cia.gov/cia/publications/ factbook/geos/iz.html. Internet. Accessed 20 May 2007.

www.ingramcontent.com/pod-product-compliance
Lightning Source LLC
Chambersburg PA
CBHW080311290526
45790CB00005B/1995